Nestlé®

TOLL HOUSE®

RECIPE COLLECTION

Welcome to the exciting world of baking and snack-making with Nestlé Toll House Morsels!

For over 50 years, Nestlé has led the way in producing the very highest quality baking ingredients, beginning with our famous Nestlé Toll House semi-sweet chocolate morsels . . . to the entire tempting array of Toll House products: peanut butter morsels, milk chocolate morsels, butterscotch flavored morsels, mint-chocolate morsels and Little Bits semi-sweet chocolate.

We've come a long, delicious way since the introduction of the Original Toll House Cookie. Today, our recipes range from quick and easy snacks to indulgently rich and elegant desserts. Whether treasured Toll House favorites or brand new ideas, all of our recipes are developed and tested by the Toll House Kitchens . . . the experts on chocolate and desserts.

Be sure to read The Toll House Kitchens Success Guide to Baking that begins on page 3. There you'll find helpful tips and guidelines to suit all your baking needs, assuring you the best possible results . . . every time.

We're sure you'll be delighted with all the luscious recipes that await you in this Nestlé Toll House Recipe Collection. Enjoy!

The Toll House Kitchens

Success Guide to Baking

"Before You Bake" Basics

1. Be sure to read the recipe completely. Make sure you have all the ingredients and baking utensils called for.

2. Remove butter, cream cheese and eggs from the refrigerator.

3. Adjust oven racks and preheat oven. Check oven temperature for accuracy with oven thermometer.

4. Prepare baking utensils according to directions.

5. Chop, grind or grate nuts; prepare or peel fruit.

6. Separate eggs if called for in recipe.

7. Measure out all ingredients and arrange in the order they are called for in the recipe.

8. Follow recipe directions and baking times exactly for best results.

Baking Tips & Techniques

Separating Eggs Tap the side of the egg on the edge of a bowl or cup to crack the shell. Pass the yolk from shell to shell, dropping the white into a cup before adding it to the other whites in the bowl. If a little yolk gets into the whites, scoop it out with part of the shell. The presence of any yolk in the whites can ruin them.

Beating Egg Whites Egg whites may be beaten with an electric mixer, rotary eggbeater, or balloon style whisk. Bowl and beater must be clean and dry because even a small amount of grease or oil can prevent the whites from whipping properly. Beat the whites slowly, gradually increasing the speed as they begin to foam. Beat only until they hold shape or point. Caution: do not beat egg whites ahead of time. They should be folded in *immediately* after they are beaten.

Whipping Cream Cream may be whipped with electric mixer, rotary eggbeater or balloon style whisk. Cream, bowl and beaters should be very cold for best results. To avoid spattering, beat slowly, gradually increasing speed as cream thickens. It's best not to whip cream too far ahead of time or it will separate slightly. If this happens, mix briefly with a wire whisk.

Blanching Almonds Place shelled nuts in a bowl. Pour in boiling water to cover and let them sit for one minute. Drain and pinch off the skins.

Toasting Nuts Preheat oven to 375°F. Spread nuts in a single layer on a baking sheet. Bake for 5 to 10 minutes, turning nuts once. Watch closely because nuts may be golden one minute and dark brown the next.

Folding Ingredients Many recipes call for folding beaten egg whites or whipped cream into another mixture. Both egg whites and whipped cream contain air in the form of many small bubbles. Folding, rather than mixing, is done to retain the air in the mixture. Start with a large bowl containing the heavier mixture. Place a portion of the egg whites or whipped cream on top of the heavier mixture. Using a circular motion with a rubber spatula, cut down through center of mixture across bottom of bowl, lifting up and over. After each fold, rotate the bowl slightly in order to incorporate the ingredients as evenly as possible. Fold in remaining egg whites or whipped cream until both mixtures are uniformly but lightly combined.

Baking Blind To bake a pie or tart shell without a filling: prick the bottom of shell with the tines of a fork. Line with aluminum foil and weight the lined shell with dried beans or uncooked rice. This makes a neater shell and will keep it from rising during the baking process.

Kneading Work the dough with a press and fold motion to evenly distribute ingredients and develop texture. Flatten the ball of dough and fold in half toward you. Press and push away with the heel of your hand. Rotate the ball a quarter turn and repeat process until dough surface is smooth.

Measuring Dry Ingredients Use the standard graded sets of four: ¼ cup, ⅓ cup, ½ cup and 1 cup. Spoon dry ingredients into measure and level off with a metal spatula.

Measuring Liquid Ingredients Use glass or plastic measuring cups with a pour spout. With the cup sitting on a flat surface, read at eye level. Fill to exactly the line indicated.

Measuring Small Quantities of Ingredients Use measuring spoons for correct measurement. For dry ingredients, fill the spoon and level off with a metal spatula. Precise measurements are essential for successful baking.

Words To Bake By

Bake To cook in an oven with dry heat. Oven should always be preheated 10–15 minutes.

Batter A mixture of flour, liquid and other ingredients that is usually thin enough to pour.

Beat To thoroughly combine ingredients and incorporate air with a rapid, regular motion. This may be done with a wire whisk, rotary eggbeater, electric mixer or food processor.

Blanch To immerse briefly in boiling water and cool quickly in ice water. Also, to pour boiling water over nuts (or tomatoes) to loosen skins.

Blend To thoroughly combine two or more ingredients.

Boil To cook in liquid in which bubbles rise continually to the surface and break.

Caramelize To heat sugar until it is melted and brown. Browning of sugar achieves a distinctive flavor.

Chill To refrigerate until cold.

Chop To cut into random sized pieces.

Cream To combine two or more ingredients by beating until the mixture is light and well blended.

Crimp To seal edges of two layers of dough with the tines of a fork.

Cut In To combine solid fat with dry ingredients by using a pastry blender or two knives in a scissor motion until particles are of the desired size.

Dash Less than ⅛ measuring teaspoonful.

Dot To distribute small amounts of butter evenly over the surface of pie filling or dough.

Drizzle To sprinkle drops of glaze or icing over food in random manner from tines of a fork or the end of a spoon.

Dust To sprinkle lightly with sugar or flour.

Flute To make a decorative scalloped edge on pie crust or pastry.

Glaze To coat with a liquid, a thin icing or a jelly either before or after food is cooked.

Grease To rub fat on surface of pan or dish to prevent sticking.

Mixing Just Until Moistened Combining dry ingredients with liquid ingredients until dry ingredients are thoroughly moistened but mixture is still lumpy.

Packed Brown Sugar Brown sugar pressed into measuring cup with a spoon. Sugar will hold its shape when cup is inverted.

Partially Set Gelatin mixture that has thickened to the consistency of unbeaten egg whites.

Full Rolling Boil To cook a mixture until it appears to rise in the pan. The surface billows rather than just bubbles.

Rounded Teaspoon To mound dough slightly in a measuring teaspoon.

Score To mark a pattern on dough with a knife, making a slight indentation but not cutting all the way through.

Simmer To cook in liquid just below the boiling point. Bubbles form slowly just below the surface.

Soft Peaks Egg whites or cream beaten to the stage where mixture forms soft rounded peaks when beaters are removed.

Stiff Peaks Egg whites or cream beaten to the stage where mixture holds stiff pointed peaks when beaters are removed.

Toss To mix lightly with a lifting motion, using two forks or spoons.

Substitution Magic

How many times has it happened to you? You're missing one item the recipe calls for and you're stuck. Don't despair; just try one of these easy sleight-of-hand substitutes.

IF THE RECIPE CALLS FOR:	YOU MAY USE:
1 teaspoon **baking powder**	¼ teaspoon baking soda+ ½ teaspoon cream of tartar.
½ cup firmly packed **brown sugar**	½ cup sugar mixed with 2 tablespoons molasses.
1 cup **buttermilk**	1 tablespoon lemon juice or vinegar and milk to make 1 cup.
½ cup **corn syrup**	½ cup sugar+2 tablespoons liquid.
1 tablespoon **cornstarch**	2 tablespoons flour OR 4 teaspoons quick-cooking tapioca.
1 cup **light cream**	⅞ cup milk+3 tablespoons butter.
1 cup sweetened **whipped cream**	4½ oz. frozen whipped topping.
1 **whole egg**	2 egg yolks+1 tablespoon water.
1 cup **cake flour**	1 cup *minus* 2 tablespoons all-purpose flour.
1 cup **honey**	1¼ cups sugar+¼ cup liquid.
1 cup **whole milk**	1 cup skim milk+2 teaspoons butter OR ½ cup evaporated milk+½ cup water.
1 teaspoon grated **orange** or **lemon rind**	½ teaspoon dried peel.

Measuring Up

These commonly used equivalent measures will simplify your recipe preparation.

GENERAL
3 teaspoons=1 tablespoon
4 tablespoons=¼ cup
5 tablespoons+1 teaspoon=⅓ cup
16 tablespoons=1 cup
2 cups=1 pint
2 pints=1 quart

BUTTER

½ oz. (⅛ stick)=1 tablespoon
1 oz. (¼ stick)=2 tablespoons
2 oz. (½ stick)=4 tablespoons
4 oz. (1 stick)=½ cup
8 oz. (2 sticks)=1 cup
16 oz. (4 sticks)=2 cups

CHOCOLATE

12 oz. morsels=1 cup melted chocolate
12 oz. morsels=2 cups whole morsels

COCONUT

3½ oz. can, flaked=1⅓ cups

CONDENSED MILK

14 oz. can=1¼ cups

CRACKERS

14 graham cracker squares=1 cup finely crushed
24 round butter crackers=1 cup finely crushed
25 vanilla wafers=1 cup finely crushed

CREAM

1 cup heavy cream=2 cups whipped cream

CREAM CHEESE

3 oz. package=6 tablespoons
8 oz. (½ lb.)=1 cup

EGGS

8–10 whites, large=1 cup egg whites
12–14 yolks, large=1 cup egg yolks

FLOUR

1 lb.=4 cups

FRUIT

1 medium lemon=3 tablespoons juice+1 tablespoon grated rind
1 medium orange=⅓ to ½ cup juice+2 tablespoons grated rind
1 lb. apples=3 medium whole or 3 cups sliced
1 lb. bananas=3 medium whole or 1½ cups mashed

NUTMEATS

4½ oz. nuts, chopped=1 cup
4 oz. almonds, shelled=⅔ cup lightly packed
1 lb. almonds in shell=⅔ cup ground

SUGAR

1 lb. brown sugar=2¼ cups
1 lb. confectioners' sugar=4½ cups sifted

Ingredient Know-How

Understanding the basic ingredients commonly used in cooking and baking—what they are and how they interact—adds interest and fun to the whole creative process. As your knowledge increases, so will your confidence in working with these versatile, everyday ingredients.

FLOUR

All-Purpose Flour is a blend of milled hard and soft wheat. This blend makes it suitable for many types of recipes. Flour is enriched to replace some of the nutrients lost in the milling process. Some flour is bleached to whiten. Unbleached and bleached flours can be used interchangeably.

Whole Wheat Flour is milled from the whole kernel of wheat. Generally 50% whole wheat flour can be substituted for all-purpose flour in recipes.

Cake Flour is milled from soft wheat and is the most highly refined flour. This is generally used in delicate cakes such as angel food or sponge cake.

Self-Rising Flour is all-purpose flour with baking powder and salt added. If used in a recipe that does not specify it, eliminate the salt and baking powder from the recipe.

FATS

Butter is made from sweet cream and contains about 80% butterfat. It is available both salted and unsalted. Butter adds a special flavor to sauteed and baked foods. Because of its low smoke point, it should not be used for deep fat frying.

Margarine is made from vegetable oils and emulsified with milk or nonfat dry milk solids. Color and salt may be added. It contains 80% fat and may be substituted for butter.

Blends are made with 40%–60% combination of butter and margarine to add the special flavor of butter at a lower price. This may be substituted for butter.

Vegetable Shortening is made of vegetable oils that have been hydrogenated under controlled conditions to change a liquid to a solid. It has no flavor and will keep at room temperature. It is ideal for deep fat frying because it has a high smoke point. It may also be used in baking.

Lard is rendered pork fat. It is used in pie crusts and makes a tender, flaky crust. The pronounced flavor of lard can interfere with some delicate food flavors.

Oils are fats that are liquid at room temperature. They are extracted from seeds or vegetables. They may be used in baking when a recipe calls for oil but may not be substituted for butter or margarine in a recipe. Oils can be used for deep fat frying.

EGGS

Eggs are most available in extra large, large and medium size. One cup of whole eggs takes about 7–8 medium, 6–7 large or 5 extra large eggs. All recipes in this book use large size eggs. Eggs should be refrigerated.

CREAM

Each type of cream available on the market has a different fat content.

Heavy Cream is often called whipping cream and contains between 36% and 40% butterfat. It will thicken when whipped.

Light Cream has a lower butterfat content (between 18–30%) than heavy cream and will not whip.

Half and Half is a mixture of half milk and half cream with a butterfat content of about 10%. This will not whip.

Sour Cream is a commercially cultured light cream that is creamy thick.

MILK

Homogenized Milk is whole milk that is mechanically treated to disperse fat evenly through milk.

Low-Fat Milk is skim milk that retains a portion of the fat (contains 0.5%–2% fat).

Skim Milk is milk that has most of the fat removed (contains less than 0.5% fat).

Cultured Buttermilk is skim milk that is soured by treating with a culture.

Evaporated Milk is canned whole milk with 60% of the water removed. It may be mixed with an equal amount of water to make whole milk.

Sweetened Condensed Milk is whole milk with 50% of the water removed and sugar added before canning. This may not be substituted for evaporated milk because it contains sugar.

Yogurt is a whole or skim milk that has been treated with a culture. It is creamy thick and more tart than sour cream.

SUGAR & SWEETENERS

Granulated Sugar is most commonly called sugar in recipes.

Confectioners' Sugar is a granulated sugar that has been ground and sifted. It is also referred to as powdered sugar.

Brown Sugar is granulated sugar with molasses added. Depending on the amount of molasses, it is labeled golden, light or dark brown.

Corn Syrup is made from corn sugar and is pourable. It comes in light and dark. It is often used in boiled frostings and candies to prevent graininess.

Honey is the nectar of plants, stored and concentrated by honey bees. It is strained to make it clear.

Maple Syrup is made by boiling down the sap from maple trees. It has a delicate flavor. Maple syrup blends are a combination of maple syrup, sugar and maple flavorings.

Molasses is the concentrated syrup remaining after granulated sugar is removed from cane. It comes in light and dark; the dark has a more intense flavor.

LEAVENING AGENTS

Baking Powder is a mixture of acid and baking soda. In the presence of moisture and heat, it releases bubbles of carbon dioxide gas that make bread, cakes and cookie doughs rise.

Baking Soda is an alkaline product that produces carbon dioxide when combined with acid ingredients such as sour milk, sour cream or molasses.

Yeast is a microscopic plant that reacts with sugar to form carbon dioxide. Yeast is available in a dry granule form, which is stored in the cupboard, and in compressed cakes, which are perishable and must be stored in the refrigerator. You can substitute one envelope of dry yeast for one cake of compressed yeast.

Baking Pan Options

If a recipe calls for a size of baking pan you don't have, chances are you can use what you *do* have on hand. Use the following list for practical substitutions. But remember, changing pan sizes will alter baking time. Smaller pans of the same shape will take *less* baking time. Shallow pans will take less time than loaf pans with higher sides. *Tip:* Keep a record of pan size changes and baking times for future use.

RECIPE CALLS FOR:	YOU MAY USE:
9×5×3-inch loaf pan	two 7½×3¾×2¼-inch loaf pans OR three 5½×3¼×2¼-inch loaf pans.
8½×4½×2½-inch loaf pan	two 5½×3¼×2¼-inch loaf pans OR one 1-lb. coffee can.
10-inch fluted tube pan	one 10×4-inch tube pan OR one 12-cup ring mold OR two 9×5×3-inch loaf pans.
13×9×2-inch pan	two 9-inch round pans OR two 8-inch round pans OR two 8-inch square pans.
One 9-inch round pan	one 8-inch square pan.
Two 9-inch round pans	three 8-inch round pans.

Chocolate: Its Care & Handling

It's no surprise that chocolate is America's favorite flavor. However, as a natural product made principally from cocoa beans, chocolate does have certain characteristics that affect the way it should be stored and used for best results.

Storing Chocolate

The key words are *cool, dry* and *low* humidity! Storage temperature should be between 60° and 78°F., with relative humidity at less than 50%. It's all right to refrigerate chocolate, but wrap it tightly so it won't absorb odors. Airtight wrapping will also prevent moisture from condensing on the chocolate when it is removed from the refrigerator. Chocolate becomes hard and brittle when cold, so allow it to come to room temperature before using.

A Tip About Milk Chocolate Morsels

Don't use milk chocolate morsels in baked desserts that do not call for melting the morsels before blending them in. The milk content causes them to become hard when they are baked. You may substitute milk chocolate morsels for semi-sweet morsels in recipes such as frostings or sauces that call for melting the morsels.

There's No Love In "Bloom," But No Harm Either

Chocolate has a high content of cocoa butter. When stored at temperatures that fluctuate from hot to cold, chocolate can develop "bloom"—a gray film caused by the cocoa butter rising to the surface. This dulls the rich brown chocolate color but it does not affect the flavor. When the chocolate melts, it regains its attractive color. Don't hesitate to use it.

MELTING CHOCOLATE PERFECTLY

Important Reminder: Even the smallest drop of moisture from a wet spoon or steam from a double boiler can cause melted chocolate to become lumpy. If this occurs, all is not lost. Stir in 1 tablespoon vegetable shortening (not butter) for every 3 ounces of chocolate. Butter is not used because it contains water. Stir continuously until the consistency is smooth and even.

Top of Stove Method: All varieties of Nestlé Toll House Morsels can be melted using this traditional method. Place the amount of morsels you want to melt in the top of a clean, dry double boiler. Place over hot (not boiling) water, stirring occasionally, until smooth. Note: water in bottom pan should be 1 inch below top pan for best results.

Microwave Method: All varieties of morsels can also be melted using a microwave oven. Simply place the amount of morsels you want to melt in a dry glass measuring cup twice the size (i.e., to melt 1 cup of morsels use a 2-cup measuring cup). Microwave on *high* for 1 minute; stir. Microwave on *high* for 30 seconds longer; stir. It is necessary to stir the morsels thoroughly to determine if they are completely melted because they retain their original shape even in the melted state. Because microwave ovens may differ in power levels, consult your "User's Guide" for specific directions for your particular model.

IF THE RECIPE CALLS FOR:	YOU MAY USE:
1 oz. (1 square) unsweetened baking chocolate	3 oz. (½ cup) Nestlé Toll House semi-sweet chocolate morsels. Decrease shortening 1 tablespoon and sugar ¼ cup.
3 oz. (3 squares) semi-sweet baking chocolate	3 oz. (½ cup) Nestlé Toll House semi-sweet chocolate morsels.
¼ cup unsweetened cocoa powder	3 oz. (½ cup) Nestlé Toll House semi-sweet chocolate morsels. Decrease shortening 1 tablespoon and sugar ¼ cup.

COOKIES

Original Toll House® Cookies ►

2¼ cups all-purpose flour
1 teaspoon baking soda
1 teaspoon salt
1 cup butter, softened
¾ cup sugar
¾ cup firmly packed
   brown sugar
1 teaspoon vanilla
   extract
2 eggs
One 12-oz. pkg. (2 cups)
   Nestlé Toll House
   semi-sweet
   chocolate morsels
1 cup chopped nuts

Preheat oven to 375°F. In small bowl, combine flour, baking soda and salt; set aside. In large bowl, combine butter, sugar, brown sugar and vanilla extract; beat until creamy. Beat in eggs. Gradually add flour mixture. Stir in Nestlé Toll House semi-sweet chocolate morsels and nuts. Drop by rounded tablespoonfuls onto ungreased cookie sheets. Bake at: 375°F. for 9–11 minutes.
Makes: 5 dozen 2¼-inch cookies.

Refrigerator Toll House Cookies: Prepare dough as directed. Divide dough in half; wrap both halves separately in waxed paper. Chill 1 hour or until firm. On waxed paper, shape each dough half into 15-inch log. Roll up in waxed paper; refrigerate for 30 minutes.* Preheat oven to 375°F. Cut each log into thirty ½-inch slices. Place on ungreased cookie sheets. Bake at 375°F. for 8–10 minutes.
Makes: 5 dozen 2¼-inch cookies.

Pan Cookie: Spread dough into greased 15½×10½×1-inch baking pan. Bake at 375°F. for 20–25 minutes. Cool completely. Cut into thirty-five 2-inch squares.

*May be stored up to 1 week in refrigerator or freeze up to 8 weeks.

Chocolate Mint Cookies ►

One 10-oz. pkg. (1½ cups)
Nestlé Toll House
mint-chocolate
morsels, divided
1 cup all-purpose flour
¾ teaspoon baking
powder
¼ teaspoon baking soda
¼ teaspoon salt
¼ cup butter, softened
6 tablespoons sugar
½ teaspoon vanilla
extract
1 egg

1 cup Nestlé Toll House
mint-chocolate
morsels, reserved
from 10-oz. pkg.
¼ cup vegetable
shortening
3 tablespoons corn
syrup
2¼ teaspoons water

Cookies: Melt over hot (not boiling) water, ½ cup Nestlé Toll House mint-chocolate morsels; stir until smooth. Set aside. In small bowl, combine flour, baking powder, baking soda and salt; set aside. In large bowl, combine butter, sugar and vanilla extract; beat until creamy. Beat in egg; blend in melted morsels. Gradually beat in flour mixture. Shape dough into ball and wrap in waxed paper. Chill about 1 hour. Preheat oven to 350°F. On lightly floured board, roll dough to ³⁄₁₆-inch thickness. Cut with 2-inch cookie cutter. Reroll remaining dough and cut out cookies. Place on ungreased cookie sheets. Bake at: 350°F. for 8–10 minutes. Cool completely on wire racks.

Glaze: Combine over hot (not boiling) water, remaining 1 cup Nestlé Toll House mint-chocolate morsels, vegetable shortening, corn syrup and water; stir until morsels are melted and mixture is smooth. Remove from heat, but keep mixture over hot water.

Dip ½ of each cookie into Glaze; shake off any excess Glaze. Place cookies on waxed-paper-lined cookie sheets. Chill until Glaze sets (about 10 minutes).
Makes: about 3½ dozen 2-inch cookies.

Note: Keep refrigerated until ready to serve.

Chocolate Mint Meltaways ▲

One 10-oz pkg. (1½ cups) Nestlé Toll House mint-chocolate morsels, divided
¾ cup butter, softened
½ cup sifted confectioners' sugar
1 egg yolk
1¼ cups all-purpose flour
2 tablespoons chopped toasted almonds

Cookies: Preheat oven to 350°F. Melt over hot (not boiling) water, 1 cup Nestlé Toll House mint-chocolate morsels; stir until smooth. Set aside. In large bowl, combine butter, confectioners' sugar and egg yolk; beat until creamy. Add melted morsels and flour; beat until well blended. Drop by heaping teaspoonfuls onto ungreased cookie sheets. Bake at: 350°F. for 8–10 minutes. Allow to stand 3 minutes before removing from cookie sheets. Cool completely on wire racks. Drizzle each cookie with ½ teaspoon Glaze; sprinkle with almonds. Chill until set. Store in airtight container in refrigerator.
Makes: about 4 dozen 1¾-inch cookies.

- -

½ cup Nestlé Toll House mint-chocolate morsels, reserved from 10-oz. pkg.
1½ tablespoons vegetable shortening

Glaze: Combine over hot (not boiling) water, remaining ½ cup Nestlé Toll House mint-chocolate morsels and vegetable shortening. Stir until morsels are melted and mixture is smooth.

◄ Chocolate Orange Granola Cookies

1 cup all-purpose flour
½ teaspoon baking powder
½ teaspoon allspice
½ teaspoon salt
⅔ cup firmly packed brown sugar
½ cup butter, softened
1 egg
1 teaspoon vanilla extract
½ teaspoon grated orange rind
1¼ cups granola cereal
One 6-oz. pkg. (1 cup) Nestlé Toll House semi-sweet chocolate morsels
½ cup flaked coconut
¼ cup chopped nuts

Preheat oven to 350°F. In small bowl, combine flour, baking powder, allspice and salt; set aside. In large bowl, combine brown sugar and butter; beat until creamy. Add egg, vanilla extract and orange rind; beat well. Gradually beat in flour mixture. Stir in granola cereal, Nestlé Toll House semi-sweet chocolate morsels, coconut and nuts. Drop by rounded tablespoonfuls onto ungreased cookie sheets. Sprinkle with additional coconut, if desired. Bake at: 350°F. for 9–11 minutes.
Makes: about 1½ dozen 2-inch cookies.

◄ Double Chocolate Cookies ✓ 6-89

2¼ cups all-purpose flour
1 teaspoon baking soda
1 teaspoon salt
1 cup butter, softened
¾ cup sugar
¾ cup firmly packed brown sugar
1 teaspoon vanilla extract
2 eggs
Two envelopes (2 oz.) Nestlé Choco-bake unsweetened baking chocolate flavor
One 12-oz. pkg. (2 cups) Nestlé Toll House semi-sweet chocolate morsels
1 cup chopped walnuts

Preheat oven to 375°F. In medium bowl, combine flour, baking soda and salt; set aside. In large bowl, combine butter, sugar, brown sugar and vanilla extract; beat until creamy. Beat in eggs and Nestlé Choco-bake unsweetened baking chocolate flavor. Gradually beat in flour mixture. Stir in Nestlé Toll House semi-sweet chocolate morsels and nuts. Drop by rounded teaspoonfuls onto ungreased cookie sheets. Bake at: 375°F. for 8–10 minutes.
Makes: about 6 dozen 2½-inch cookies.

Chocolate-Dipped Sandwich Macaroons ►

One 12-oz. pkg. (2 cups)
    Nestlé Toll House
    Little Bits semi-
    sweet chocolate,
    divided
1½ cups blanched
    almonds, finely
    ground
1½ cups sifted
    confectioners' sugar
3 egg whites, at room
    temperature
⅓ cup jam or jelly
2 tablespoons vegetable
    shortening

Preheat oven to 350°F. In small bowl, combine 1 cup Nestlé Toll House Little Bits semi-sweet chocolate, almonds and confectioners' sugar; set aside. In large bowl, beat egg whites until stiff peaks form. Fold in almond mixture. Drop by level teaspoonfuls onto parchment-paper-lined cookie sheets. Bake at: 350°F. for 8–10 minutes. Cool 5 minutes. Remove from paper to wire racks; cool completely. Spread ¼ teaspoon jam or jelly on flat side of one cookie; top with second cookie. Repeat with remaining cookies. Set aside. Combine over hot (not boiling) water, remaining 1 cup Nestlé Toll House Little Bits semi-sweet chocolate and vegetable shortening. Stir until morsels are melted and mixture is smooth. Remove from heat, but keep over hot water. Dip ½ of each sandwich cookie into chocolate. Place on waxed-paper-lined cookie sheets. Chill until set. Makes: about 4 dozen 1½-inch cookies.

Mocha Walnut Cookies

One 12-oz. pkg. (2 cups)
    Nestlé Toll House
    semi-sweet
    chocolate morsels,
    divided
2 tablespoons Nescafé
    Classic instant
    coffee
2 teaspoons boiling
    water
1¼ cups all-purpose flour
¾ teaspoon baking soda
½ teaspoon salt
½ cup butter, softened
½ cup sugar
½ cup firmly packed
    brown sugar
1 egg
½ cup chopped walnuts

Preheat oven to 350°F. Melt over hot (not boiling) water, ½ cup Nestlé Toll House semi-sweet chocolate morsels; stir until smooth. Cool to room temperature. In small cup, dissolve Nescafé Classic instant coffee in boiling water; set aside. In small bowl, combine flour, baking soda and salt; set aside. In large bowl, combine butter, sugar, brown sugar and coffee; beat until creamy. Add egg and melted morsels; mix well. Gradually beat in flour mixture. Stir in remaining 1½ cups Nestlé Toll House semi-sweet chocolate morsels and walnuts. Drop by rounded tablespoonfuls onto ungreased cookie sheets. Bake at: 350°F. for 10–12 minutes. Allow to stand 2–3 minutes before removing from cookie sheets; cool completely on wire racks. Makes: about 2 dozen 3-inch cookies.

▲ Milk Chocolate Florentine Cookies

⅔ cup butter
2 cups quick oats,
  uncooked
1 cup sugar
⅔ cup all-purpose flour
¼ cup corn syrup
¼ cup milk
1 teaspoon vanilla
  extract
¼ teaspoon salt
One 11½-oz. pkg. (2 cups)
  Nestlé Toll House
  milk chocolate
  morsels

Preheat oven to 375°F. Melt butter in medium saucepan over low heat. Remove from heat. Stir in oats, sugar, flour, corn syrup, milk, vanilla extract and salt; mix well. Drop by level teaspoonfuls, about 3 inches apart, onto foil-lined cookie sheets. Spread thin with rubber spatula. Bake at: 375°F for 5–7 minutes. Cool completely. Peel foil away from cookies. Melt over hot (not boiling) water, Nestlé Toll House milk chocolate morsels; stir until smooth. Spread chocolate on flat side of ½ the cookies. Top with remaining cookies.
Makes: about 3½ dozen sandwich cookies.

Oatmeal Extravaganzas

1 cup + 2 tablespoons
  all-purpose flour
1½ teaspoons baking
  powder
½ teaspoon salt
1 cup + 2 tablespoons
  firmly packed brown
  sugar
¾ cup butter, softened
2 teaspoons vanilla
  extract
¼ cup water
2 cups quick oats,
  uncooked
One 12-oz. pkg. (2 cups)
  Nestlé Toll House
  semi-sweet
  chocolate morsels

Preheat oven to 375°F. In small bowl, combine flour, baking powder and salt; set aside. In large bowl, combine brown sugar, butter and vanilla extract; beat until creamy. Gradually blend in flour mixture alternately with water. Stir in oats and Nestlé Toll House semi-sweet chocolate morsels. Spread in greased 9-inch square baking pan. Bake at: 375°F. for 30 minutes. Cool completely; cut into 1½-inch squares. Makes: 3 dozen 1½-inch squares.

Irish Coffee Brownies

One 11½-oz. pkg. (2 cups)
  Nestlé Toll House
  milk chocolate
  morsels, divided
½ cup butter
½ cup sugar
2 eggs
1 teaspoon vanilla
  extract
2 tablespoons Irish
  whiskey
2 teaspoons Nescafé
  Classic instant
  coffee
1 cup all-purpose flour

Preheat oven to 350°F. In small saucepan over low heat, combine 1 cup Nestlé Toll House milk chocolate morsels and butter; stir until morsels are melted and mixture is smooth. Cool to room temperature. In large bowl, combine sugar and eggs; beat until thick and lemon colored. Gradually beat in chocolate mixture and vanilla extract. In cup, combine Irish whiskey and Nescafé Classic instant coffee; stir until dissolved. Add to chocolate mixture. Gradually blend in flour. Pour into foil-lined 8-inch square baking pan. Bake at: 350°F. for 25–30 minutes. Immediately sprinkle remaining 1 cup Nestlé Toll House milk chocolate morsels on top. Let stand until morsels are shiny and soft; spread evenly. Cool completely; cut into 2-inch squares.
Makes: sixteen 2-inch brownies.

Oatmeal Scotchies™ ▶

1 cup all-purpose flour
1 teaspoon baking soda
½ teaspoon salt
½ teaspoon cinnamon
1 cup butter, softened
¾ cup sugar
¾ cup firmly packed brown sugar
2 eggs
1 teaspoon vanilla extract
3 cups oats, uncooked (Quick or Old Fashioned)
One 12-oz. pkg. (2 cups) Nestlé Toll House butterscotch flavored morsels

Preheat oven to 375°F. In small bowl, combine flour, baking soda, salt and cinnamon; set aside. In large bowl, combine butter, sugar, brown sugar, eggs and vanilla extract; beat until creamy. Gradually add flour mixture. Stir in oats and Nestlé Toll House butterscotch flavored morsels. Drop by level tablespoonfuls onto ungreased cookie sheets. Bake at: 375°F. for 7–8 minutes for chewier cookies, 9–10 minutes for crisper cookies.
Makes: about 4 dozen 3-inch cookies.

Oatmeal Scotchie Pan Cookie: Spread the dough into greased 15½×10½×1-inch baking pan. Bake at 375°F. for 20–25 minutes. Cool completely. Cut into thirty-five 2-inch squares.

Butterscotch Lemon Cookies ▶

1½ cups all-purpose flour
2 teaspoons baking powder
½ teaspoon salt
¾ cup sugar
½ cup butter, softened
1 egg
2 tablespoons milk
1 tablespoon lemon juice
1 teaspoon grated lemon rind
¾ of 12-oz pkg. (1½ cups) Nestlé Toll House butterscotch flavored morsels

Preheat oven to 375°F. In small bowl, combine flour, baking powder and salt; set aside. In large bowl, combine sugar and butter; beat well. Add egg, milk, lemon juice and lemon rind; beat well.* Gradually beat in flour mixture. Stir in Nestlé Toll House butterscotch flavored morsels. Drop by rounded tablespoonfuls onto greased cookie sheets. Bake at: 375°F. for 8–10 minutes. Allow to stand 2 minutes before removing from cookie sheets. Cool completely on wire racks.
Makes: about 1½ dozen 3-inch cookies.

*Mixture will appear curdled.

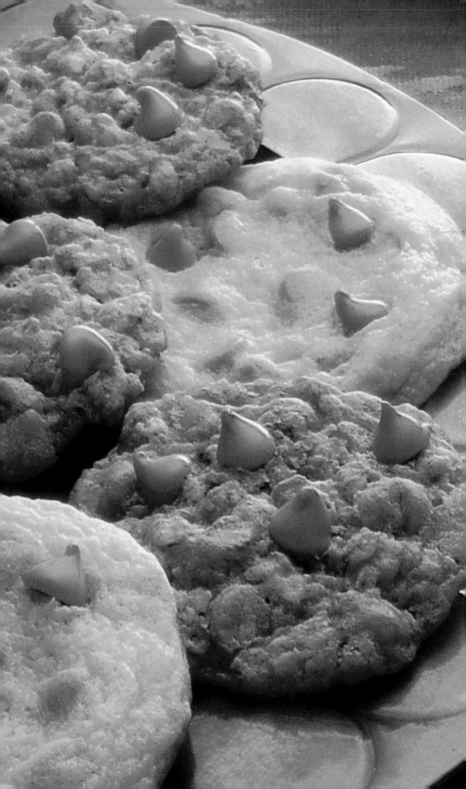

Chocolate Raspberry Coconut Squares ▼

1 cup all-purpose flour
¼ cup firmly packed brown sugar
½ cup butter, softened

Cookie Base: Preheat oven to 350°F. In medium bowl, combine flour and brown sugar. With pastry blender or 2 knives, cut in butter until mixture resembles fine crumbs. Press into greased 9-inch square baking pan. Bake at: 350°F. for 20 minutes.

1 cup sweetened condensed milk
½ cup all-purpose flour
½ teaspoon baking powder
¼ teaspoon salt
2 eggs
One 6-oz. pkg. (1 cup) Nestlé Toll House semi-sweet chocolate morsels
One 3½-oz. can (1⅓ cups) flaked coconut, divided
½ cup chopped pecans
½ cup raspberry preserves

Topping: In large bowl, combine sweetened condensed milk, flour, baking powder, salt and eggs; mix well. Stir in Nestlé Toll House semi-sweet chocolate morsels, 1 cup coconut and pecans. Pour over baked Cookie Base. Bake at: 350°F. for 25 minutes. Remove from oven. Spread preserves over top of bars. Sprinkle with remaining ⅓ cup coconut. Cool completely. Cut into 1½-inch squares. Makes: 3 dozen 1½-inch squares.

Butterscotch Apricot Streusel Bars

One 8-oz. pkg. dried
  apricots
1½ cups water

Filling: In medium saucepan, combine apricots and water. Cook over medium heat, stirring occasionally, until water evaporates and mixture is thickened. Set aside.

2 cups whole wheat
  flour, divided
1⅔ cups quick oats,
  uncooked
¾ teaspoon salt
½ teaspoon baking soda
¾ cup molasses
½ cup butter, softened
One 6-oz. pkg. (1 cup)
  Nestlé Toll House
  butterscotch
  flavored morsels

Cookie Layer: Preheat oven to 375°F. In small bowl, combine 1¾ cups flour, oats, salt and baking soda; set aside. In large bowl, combine molasses and butter; beat until creamy. Gradually beat in flour mixture. Remove 1 cup of mixture and place in small bowl; set aside. Press remaining mixture into foil-lined 13×9-inch baking pan. Top with Filling; set aside. Add remaining ¼ cup flour to reserved mixture; stir until crumbs form. Stir in Nestlé Toll House butterscotch flavored morsels. Sprinkle crumb mixture on top. Bake at: 375°F. for 20–25 minutes. Cool completely. Cut into 2×1½-inch bars.
Makes: 3 dozen 2×1½-inch bars.

Spice Islands Butterscotch Bars

1¾ cups all-purpose flour
1 teaspoon ground
  ginger
½ teaspoon baking soda
¼ teaspoon ground
  cloves
¾ cup + 2 tablespoons
  vegetable oil
½ cup molasses
¼ cup firmly packed
  brown sugar
1 egg
1 cup chopped nuts
One 6-oz. pkg. (1 cup)
  Nestlé Toll House
  butterscotch
  flavored morsels
Confectioners' sugar

Preheat oven to 350°F. In small bowl, combine flour, ginger, baking soda and cloves; set aside. In large bowl, combine vegetable oil, molasses, brown sugar and egg; beat well. Gradually beat in flour mixture. Stir in nuts and Nestlé Toll House butterscotch flavored morsels. Pour into greased 13×9-inch baking pan. Bake at: 350°F. for 20–25 minutes. Cool completely. Sprinkle with confectioners' sugar. Cut into 2×1-inch bars. Makes: 4½ dozen 2×1-inch bars.

handwritten: ✓ 12 40

Minty Fudge Brownies ►

1¼ cups all-purpose flour
½ teaspoon baking soda
½ teaspoon salt
1 cup sugar
½ cup butter
3 tablespoons water
One 10-oz. pkg. (1½ cups)
    Nestlé Toll House
    mint-chocolate
    morsels
1½ teaspoons vanilla
    extract
3 eggs
1 cup chopped nuts

Preheat oven to 325°F. In small bowl, combine flour, baking soda and salt; set aside. In medium saucepan, combine sugar, butter and water; bring *just to a boil*. Remove from heat. Add Nestlé Toll House mint-chocolate morsels and vanilla extract; stir until morsels are melted and mixture is smooth. Transfer to large bowl. Add eggs, 1 at a time, beating well after each addition. Gradually blend in flour mixture. Stir in nuts. Spread into greased 13×9-inch baking pan. Bake at: 325°F. for 30–35 minutes. Cool; cut into 1½-inch squares. Garnish with walnut halves, if desired. Makes: 4 dozen 1½-inch brownies.

Black & White Cheesecake Brownies ►

handwritten: ✓ 10-93 8080

One 12-oz. pkg. (2 cups)
    Nestlé Toll House
    Little Bits semi-
    sweet chocolate,
    divided
½ cup sugar
¼ cup butter, softened
2 eggs
1 teaspoon vanilla
    extract
½ teaspoon salt
⅔ cup all-purpose flour

Brownie Base: Preheat oven to 350°F. Melt over hot (not boiling) water, 1¼ cups Nestlé Toll House Little Bits semi-sweet chocolate; stir until smooth. Set aside. In large bowl, combine sugar and butter; beat until creamy. Add eggs, vanilla extract and salt; mix well. Add melted morsels and flour; mix well. Spread into foil-lined 9-inch square baking pan.

One 8-oz. pkg. cream
    cheese, softened
½ cup sugar
2 tablespoons butter,
    softened
2 eggs
2 tablespoons milk
1 tablespoon all-
    purpose flour
½ teaspoon almond
    extract
¾ cup Nestlé Toll House
    Little Bits semi-
    sweet chocolate,
    reserved from 12-oz.
    pkg.

Cheesecake Topping: In large bowl, combine cream cheese, sugar and butter; beat until creamy. Add eggs, milk, flour and almond extract; beat well. Stir in remaining ¾ cup Nestlé Toll House Little Bits semi-sweet chocolate. Pour over Brownie Base. Bake at: 350°F. for 40–45 minutes. Cool completely; cut into 2¼-inch squares.
Makes: sixteen 2¼-inch brownies.

No-Bake Butterscotch Snack Bars ▶

One 14-oz. box circle
   shaped bran cereal,
   coarsely crushed
1 cup raisins
⅔ cup corn syrup
3 tablespoons butter
One 6-oz. pkg. (1 cup)
   Nestlé Toll House
   butterscotch
   flavored morsels

In large bowl, combine cereal and raisins; set aside. In heavy gauge saucepan, combine corn syrup and butter. Bring to *full rolling boil* over medium heat, stirring occasionally. Remove from heat. Add Nestlé Toll House butterscotch flavored morsels; stir until morsels are melted and mixture is smooth. Pour over cereal; mix well. Press into foil-lined 13×9-inch pan. Chill until set (about 10 minutes). Cut into 2×1-inch bars. Makes: 4½ dozen 2×1-inch bars.

No-Bake Fudge Brownies

One 12-oz. pkg. (2 cups)
   Nestlé Toll House
   semi-sweet
   chocolate morsels
One 14-oz. can sweetened
   condensed milk
One 8½-oz. pkg. chocolate
   wafers, finely
   crushed
1 cup chopped nuts,
   divided

Melt over hot (not boiling) water, Nestlé Toll House semi-sweet chocolate morsels; stir until smooth. Add sweetened condensed milk, chocolate wafer crumbs and ½ cup nuts; stir until well blended. Press into foil-lined 8-inch square pan. Press remaining ½ cup nuts into top of brownie. Let stand at room temperature until firm. Cut into 2-inch squares.
Makes: sixteen 2-inch brownies.

No-Bake Chocolate
Peanut Butter Snack Bars ▶

One 16-oz. pkg. granola
   cereal
⅔ cup corn syrup
3 tablespoons butter
½ of 12-oz. pkg.
   (1 cup) Nestlé Toll
   House peanut butter
   morsels
One 6-oz. pkg. (1 cup)
   Nestlé Toll House
   semi-sweet
   chocolate morsels

Place cereal in large bowl; set aside. In heavy gauge saucepan, combine corn syrup and butter. Bring to *full rolling boil* over medium heat, stirring occasionally. Remove from heat. Add Nestlé Toll House peanut butter morsels; stir until morsels are melted and mixture is smooth. Pour over cereal; mix well. Press into foil-lined 13×9-inch pan. Melt over hot (not boiling) water, Nestlé Toll House semi-sweet chocolate morsels; stir until smooth. Spread evenly on top. Chill until set (about 10 minutes). Cut into 2×1-inch bars.
Makes: 4½ dozen 2×1-inch bars.

◄ Maple Walnut Bars

1 cup all-purpose flour
½ teaspoon baking powder
½ cup butter, softened
½ cup firmly packed brown sugar
1 egg
½ cup maple flavored syrup
1 teaspoon vanilla extract
One 12-oz. pkg. (2 cups) Nestlé Toll House Little Bits semi-sweet chocolate, divided
1 cup finely chopped walnuts, divided

Preheat oven to 350°F. In small bowl, combine flour and baking powder; set aside. In large bowl, combine butter and brown sugar; beat until creamy. Add egg, maple flavored syrup and vanilla extract; beat well. Gradually beat in flour mixture. Stir in 1 cup Nestlé Toll House Little Bits semi-sweet chocolate and ⅔ cup walnuts. Spread into greased 13×9-inch baking pan. Bake at: 350°F. for 25 minutes. Remove from oven; immediately sprinkle with remaining 1 cup Nestlé Toll House Little Bits semi-sweet chocolate. Let stand about 3 minutes until morsels become shiny and soft; spread evenly over top of bars. Sprinkle with remaining ⅓ cup walnuts. Cool completely. Cut into 2×1-inch bars.
Makes: 4½ dozen 2×1-inch bars.

◄ Peanut Butter Carrot Bars

1⅓ cups all-purpose flour
½ teaspoon baking powder
½ teaspoon cinnamon
¾ cup butter, softened
¾ cup sugar
2 eggs
One 12-oz. pkg. (2 cups) Nestlé Toll House peanut butter morsels
1½ cups shredded carrots
Confectioners' sugar

Preheat oven to 350°F. In small bowl, combine flour, baking powder and cinnamon; set aside. In large bowl, combine butter and sugar; beat until creamy. Add eggs; beat well. Gradually beat in flour mixture. Stir in Nestlé Toll House peanut butter morsels and carrots. Spread into greased and floured 13×9-inch baking pan. Bake at: 350°F. for 25–30 minutes. Cool completely. Sprinkle with confectioners' sugar. Cut into 2×1-inch bars.
Makes: 4½ dozen 2×1-inch bars.

PIES

Butterscotch Rum Chiffon Pie

1 envelope unflavored
    gelatin
¼ cup cold water
4 eggs, separated
½ cup milk
½ teaspoon salt
One 6-oz. pkg. (1 cup)
    Nestlé Toll House
    butterscotch
    flavored morsels
1 tablespoon rum
¼ cup sugar
½ cup heavy cream,
    whipped
One 9-inch *baked* pie
    shell*

In cup, combine gelatin and cold water; set aside. Combine over hot (not boiling) water, egg yolks, milk and salt. Cook, stirring constantly with wire whisk, until slightly thickened. Remove from heat. Stir in gelatin until dissolved. Add Nestlé Toll House butterscotch flavored morsels and rum; stir until morsels are melted and mixture is smooth. Transfer to large bowl. Chill, stirring occasionally, until mixture mounds slightly when dropped from spoon (about 20–30 minutes). In 1½-quart bowl, beat egg whites until foamy. Gradually add sugar; beat until stiff peaks form. Fold egg whites and whipped cream into butterscotch mixture. Pour into prepared pie shell.* Chill until firm (about 4 hours). Makes: one 9-inch pie.

*If using frozen pie shell, it's necessary to use deep dish style.

Minty Mousse Pie au Chocolat

6 tablespoons sugar,
    divided
2 tablespoons +
    2 teaspoons
    cornstarch
⅔ of 10-oz. pkg. (1 cup)
    Nestlé Toll House
    mint-chocolate
    morsels
1½ cups milk
1 cup heavy cream
One 9-inch prepared
    graham cracker
    crust

In medium heavy gauge saucepan, combine 4 tablespoons sugar, cornstarch and Nestlé Toll House mint-chocolate morsels. Gradually stir in milk. Cook, stirring constantly, over medium heat until mixture *boils*. Boil 1 *minute*; remove from heat. Transfer to large bowl; cover surface of chocolate mixture with plastic wrap. Cool to room temperature (20–30 minutes). In medium bowl, combine heavy cream with remaining 2 tablespoons sugar; beat until stiff. Remove plastic wrap from chocolate; beat well. Fold in whipped cream. Spoon into crust. Chill until firm (about 2–3 hours). Makes: one 9-inch pie.

▼ Frozen Strawberry Fudge Pie

**Two 10-oz. pkgs. frozen
quick thaw
strawberries,
thawed and drained**
¼ cup corn syrup
**One 12-oz. container frozen
non-dairy whipped
topping, thawed,
divided**
**One 9-inch prepared
chocolate crumb
crust**
**One 6-oz. pkg. (1 cup)
Nestlé Toll House
semi-sweet
chocolate morsels**

Place drained strawberries in blender or food processor container. Cover; process until pureed. Transfer to large bowl. Add corn syrup; mix well. Fold in 2 cups whipped topping. Spoon into crust. Freeze until firm (about 1½ hours). Combine over hot (not boiling) water, 1 cup whipped topping and Nestlé Toll House semi-sweet chocolate morsels; stir until morsels are melted and mixture is smooth. Spread evenly over strawberry layer. Freeze until firm (about 1½ hours). Garnish with remaining whipped topping and chocolate-dipped strawberries, if desired.
Makes: one 9-inch pie.

Chocolate Chip Tarts à l'Orange

One 15-oz. container
ricotta cheese
2 eggs
¼ cup sugar
2 tablespoons butter,
melted
½ teaspoon vanilla
extract
One 6-oz. pkg. (1 cup)
Nestlé Toll House
semi-sweet
chocolate morsels
Two 4-oz. pkgs. single
serve graham crusts
Two 11-oz. cans mandarin
oranges, drained
¼ cup apricot preserves

Preheat oven to 350°F. In large bowl, combine ricotta cheese, eggs, sugar, butter and vanilla extract; beat well. Stir in Nestlé Toll House semi-sweet chocolate morsels. Spoon ¼ cup into each crust. Place on cookie sheet. Bake at: 350°F. for 20–25 minutes. Centers will be soft. Cool completely. Arrange orange segments on top of each tart. In small saucepan over low heat, melt apricot preserves. Brush orange segments with preserves. Chill.
Makes: 12 tarts.

Frozen Mocha Mousse Pie

1 to 1½ teaspoons
Taster's Choice
freeze dried coffee
1 teaspoon boiling water
½ of 11½-oz. pkg.
(1 cup) Nestlé Toll
House milk
chocolate morsels
¾ cup heavy cream,
divided
2 egg whites
One 9-inch prepared
graham cracker
crust
Whipped cream
(optional)

In cup, dissolve Taster's Choice freeze dried coffee in boiling water. Combine over hot (not boiling) water, Nestlé Toll House milk chocolate morsels, ¼ cup heavy cream and coffee; stir until morsels are melted and mixture is smooth. Transfer to large bowl; cool 10–15 minutes. In 1½-quart bowl, beat egg whites until stiff peaks form. Fold into chocolate mixture. In small bowl, beat remaining ½ cup heavy cream until stiff peaks form; fold into chocolate mixture. Spoon into crust. Freeze until firm (about 4 hours). Garnish with whipped cream, if desired.
Makes: one 9-inch pie.

▲ Cafe Cream Pie

One 6-oz. pkg. (1 cup)
  Nestlé Toll House
  semi-sweet
  chocolate morsels
1 tablespoon vegetable
  shortening
1½ cups finely chopped
  nuts

Choco-Nut Crust: Combine over hot (not boiling) water, Nestlé Toll House semi-sweet chocolate morsels and shortening; stir until morsels are melted and mixture is smooth. Stir in nuts. Spread evenly on bottom and up sides (not over rim) of foil-lined 9-inch pie pan. Chill until firm (about 1 hour). Lift chocolate crust out of pan; peel off foil and place crust back into pie pan or onto serving plate. Chill until ready to use.

½ lb. marshmallows
  (about 40 large)
⅓ cup milk
¼ teaspoon salt
3 tablespoons coffee
  flavored liqueur
3 tablespoons vodka
1½ cups heavy cream,
  whipped

Filling: Combine over hot (not boiling) water, marshmallows, milk and salt; stir until marshmallows are melted. Remove from heat. Add coffee flavored liqueur and vodka; stir until well blended. Transfer to medium bowl. Chill until slightly thickened (about 45–60 minutes), stirring occasionally. Gently fold in whipped cream. Pour into prepared Choco-Nut Crust; chill until firm (about 1 hour). Garnish as desired. Makes: one 9-inch pie.

▲ Toll House™ Pie

2 eggs
½ cup all-purpose flour
½ cup sugar
½ cup firmly packed
    brown sugar
1 cup butter, melted and
    cooled to room
    temperature
One 6-oz. pkg. (1 cup)
    Nestlé Toll House
    semi-sweet
    chocolate morsels
1 cup chopped walnuts
One 9-inch unbaked pie
    shell*
    Whipped cream or ice
    cream (optional)

Preheat oven to 325°F. In large bowl, beat eggs until foamy. Add flour, sugar and brown sugar; beat until well blended. Blend in melted butter. Stir in Nestlé Toll House semi-sweet chocolate morsels and walnuts. Pour into pie shell.* Bake at: 325°F. for 1 hour. Serve warm with whipped cream or ice cream, if desired. Makes: one 9-inch pie.

*If using frozen pie shell, it's necessary to use deep dish style, thawed. Place on cookie sheet and bake additional 10 minutes.

Recipe may be doubled. Bake two pies; freeze one for later use.

▼ Quick Butterscotch Ice Cream Pie

1½ cups chopped toasted pecans, divided
1 cup graham cracker crumbs
⅓ cup butter, melted

Crust: In small bowl, combine ½ cup pecans, graham cracker crumbs and butter; mix well. Press crumb mixture into 9-inch pie plate; set aside.

½ cup sugar
½ cup water
One 6-oz. pkg. (1 cup) Nestlé Toll House butterscotch flavored morsels
2 eggs
½ teaspoon salt
⅛ teaspoon nutmeg
1¾ cups heavy cream, whipped

Filling: In small saucepan, combine sugar and water. Bring to *boil* over medium heat; *boil 3 minutes.* Remove from heat. In blender container, combine Nestlé Toll House butterscotch flavored morsels and sugar mixture; cover and blend at high speed 30 seconds. Add eggs, salt and nutmeg; cover and blend at high speed 1 minute. Cool to room temperature. Fold into whipped cream. Spoon ½ of filling into prepared Crust. Sprinkle ½ cup pecans on top. Spoon remaining filling on top. Garnish with remaining ½ cup pecans. Freeze several hours or until firm.
Makes: one 9-inch pie.

▲ Chocolate Cream Strawberry Tart

Pastry for one crust 9-inch pie

Tart Shell: Preheat oven to 425°F. Fit pastry dough into 9-inch removable-bottom tart pan. Press dough firmly into bottom and sides of pan; trim edges. Line pastry dough with foil; weight with dried beans. Bake at: 425°F. for 10 minutes. Remove foil; bake additional 2–3 minutes. Cool completely. Remove from pan.

¼ cup sugar
3 tablespoons all-purpose flour
¼ teaspoon salt
1 cup milk
4 egg yolks
One 6-oz. pkg. (1 cup) Nestlé Toll House semi-sweet chocolate morsels
2 tablespoons butter
2 teaspoons vanilla extract
2 pints strawberries, washed and hulled
2 tablespoons strawberry jelly

Pastry Cream: In medium saucepan, combine sugar, flour and salt. Gradually add milk. Cook over low heat, stirring constantly, until mixture *boils. Boil 2 minutes*, stirring constantly; remove from heat. Beat in egg yolks; return to heat and cook 1 minute longer. Remove from heat. Add Nestlé Toll House semi-sweet chocolate morsels, butter and vanilla extract. Stir until morsels are melted and mixture is smooth. Place plastic wrap on surface of pastry cream. Chill 30 minutes. Stir; spread evenly into baked Tart Shell. Arrange strawberries on top. In small saucepan over low heat, melt strawberry jelly. Brush over strawberries. Chill several hours. Let stand at room temperature 15 minutes before serving.
Makes: one 9-inch tart.

Nutty Chocolate Sour Cream Pie

4 eggs
²/₃ cup sour cream
²/₃ cup firmly packed
    brown sugar
¹/₄ cup honey
1 teaspoon vanilla
    extract
2 cups chopped pecans
One 6-oz. pkg. (1 cup)
    Nestlé Toll House
    semi-sweet
    chocolate morsels
One 9-inch unbaked pie
    shell*
    Whipped cream
    (optional)

Preheat oven to 350°F. In large bowl, combine eggs, sour cream, brown sugar, honey and vanilla extract; beat well. Stir in pecans and Nestlé Toll House semi-sweet chocolate morsels. Pour into prepared pie shell.* Bake at: 350°F. for 40–45 minutes. Serve warm with whipped cream, if desired.
Makes: one 9-inch pie.

*If using frozen pie shell, it's necessary to use deep dish style, thawed. Place on cookie sheet and bake additional 10 minutes.

Mocha Cheese Pie

One 6-oz. pkg. (1 cup)
    Nestlé Toll House
    semi-sweet
    chocolate morsels
1 tablespoon Taster's
    Choice freeze dried
    coffee
1 tablespoon boiling
    water
Two 8-oz. pkgs. cream
    cheese, softened
¹/₃ cup sugar
3 eggs
¹/₄ cup heavy cream
One 9-inch unbaked pie
    shell*
    Sweetened whipped
    cream (optional)

Preheat oven to 350°F. Melt over hot (not boiling) water, Nestlé Toll House semi-sweet chocolate morsels; stir until smooth. Set aside. In cup, dissolve Taster's Choice freeze dried coffee in boiling water. In large bowl, combine cream cheese and sugar; beat until smooth. Add eggs, 1 at a time, beating well after each addition. Add melted morsels and coffee; mix well. Blend in heavy cream. Pour into prepared pie shell.* Bake at: 350°F. for 35–40 minutes. Turn oven off. Let stand in oven with door ajar 15 minutes. Remove. Cool completely; chill. Let stand at room temperature 30 minutes before serving. Garnish with sweetened whipped cream, if desired.
Makes: one 9-inch pie.

*If using frozen pie shell, it's necessary to use deep dish style, thawed. Place on cookie sheet and bake additional 10 minutes.

CAKES

√ 1-91

Cheesecake Cupcakes ▶

Two 3-oz. pkgs. cream
    cheese, softened
  ¼ cup sugar
  1 egg
  ⅛ teaspoon salt
One 6-oz. pkg. (1 cup)
    Nestlé Toll House
    semi-sweet
    chocolate morsels,
    divided

Filling: In medium bowl, combine cream cheese, sugar, egg and salt; beat until creamy. Stir in ½ cup Nestlé Toll House semi-sweet chocolate morsels. Set aside.

  ½ cup Nestlé Toll House
    semi-sweet
    chocolate morsels,
    reserved from 6-oz.
    pkg.
1½ cups all-purpose flour
  1 teaspoon baking soda
  ½ teaspoon salt
  ½ cup sugar
  ⅓ cup vegetable oil
  1 egg
  1 teaspoon vanilla
    extract
  1 cup water
    Confectioners' sugar

Cake: Preheat oven to 350°F. Melt over hot (not boiling) water, remaining ½ cup Nestlé Toll House semi-sweet chocolate morsels; stir until smooth. Remove from heat; set aside. In small bowl, combine flour, baking soda and salt; set aside. In large bowl, combine sugar, vegetable oil, egg and vanilla extract; beat well. Stir in melted morsels. Gradually beat in flour mixture alternately with water. Spoon ½ of batter into 16 paper-lined cupcake pans. Spoon 1 slightly rounded tablespoon Filling over batter. Spoon remaining batter over Filling. Bake at: 350°F. for 23–25 minutes. Cool 5 minutes; remove from pans. Cool completely on wire racks. Sprinkle with confectioners' sugar. Makes: 16 cupcakes.

▲ Chocolate Hazelnut Gâteau

One 12-oz. pkg. (2 cups) Nestlé Toll House semi-sweet chocolate morsels, divided
¾ cup sugar
⅔ cup butter, softened
3 eggs, separated
1 teaspoon vanilla extract
½ teaspoon salt
¾ cup all-purpose flour
¼ cup milk
⅔ cup ground toasted hazelnuts

Cake: Preheat oven to 350°F. Melt over hot (not boiling) water, 1 cup Nestlé Toll House semi-sweet chocolate morsels; stir until smooth. Set aside. In large bowl, combine sugar and butter; beat until creamy. Beat in melted morsels, egg yolks, vanilla extract and salt. Gradually add flour and milk; beat well. Stir in hazelnuts. In 1½-quart bowl, beat egg whites until stiff peaks form. Fold into chocolate batter. Spread into greased 9-inch round springform pan. Bake at: 350°F. for 25–30 minutes. Cool 10 minutes; remove sides of pan. Cool completely. Pour Glaze over cake, covering top and sides. Garnish as desired. Makes: one cake.

3 tablespoons butter
2 tablespoons corn syrup
1 tablespoon water
1 cup Nestlé Toll House semi-sweet chocolate morsels, reserved from 12-oz. pkg.

Glaze: In small saucepan, combine butter, corn syrup and water; cook over low heat, stirring constantly. Bring to *boil*; remove from heat. Add remaining 1 cup Nestlé Toll House semi-sweet chocolate morsels; stir until morsels are melted and mixture is smooth. Cool to room temperature.

Butterscotch Fruit Spice Cake

2 cups all-purpose flour
1 tablespoon baking
  powder
¾ teaspoon salt
½ teaspoon nutmeg
¼ teaspoon ginger
¼ teaspoon cloves
1¼ cups vegetable oil
1 cup sugar
¼ cup firmly packed
  brown sugar
4 eggs
1 teaspoon rum extract
One 8-oz. can juice packed
  crushed pineapple,
  drained, reserving
  ¼ cup juice
½ cup finely chopped
  dried apricots
One 6-oz. pkg. (1 cup)
  Nestlé Toll House
  butterscotch
  flavored morsels

Cake: Preheat oven to 350°F. In medium bowl, combine flour, baking powder, salt, nutmeg, ginger and cloves; set aside. In large bowl, combine vegetable oil, sugar, brown sugar, eggs and rum extract; beat until well blended. Gradually beat in flour mixture. Stir in pineapple, apricots and Nestlé Toll House butterscotch flavored morsels. Pour into greased and floured 10-inch fluted tube pan. Bake at: 350°F. for 50–60 minutes. Cool 15 minutes; remove from pan. Pierce cake evenly all over with toothpick. Brush cake with Glaze. Cool completely on wire rack.
Makes: one tube cake.

. . . .

¼ cup reserved
  pineapple juice
½ cup sifted
  confectioners' sugar

Glaze: In small bowl, combine reserved ¼ cup pineapple juice and confectioners' sugar; stir until blended.

▲ Strawberry Chocolate Shortcake

One 6-oz. pkg. (1 cup)
   Nestlé Toll House
   semi-sweet
   chocolate morsels,
   divided
½ cup milk
2 cups all-purpose flour
¼ cup + 2 tablespoons
   sugar, divided
1 tablespoon baking
   powder
1 teaspoon salt
½ cup butter

Preheat oven to 450°F. Combine over hot (not boiling) water, ½ cup Nestlé Toll House semi-sweet chocolate morsels and milk. Stir until morsels are melted and mixture is smooth. Set aside. In large bowl, combine flour, 2 tablespoons sugar, baking powder and salt. With pastry blender or 2 knives, cut in butter until mixture resembles coarse crumbs. Add chocolate mixture; stir until blended. Knead in remaining ½ cup Nestlé Toll House semi-sweet chocolate morsels. On floured board, roll dough to ½-inch thickness. Cut dough into 8 pieces with 3-inch round cookie cutter. Place on ungreased cookie sheet. Bake at: 450°F. for 8–10 minutes. Cool completely on wire racks.

2 pints strawberries,
   washed, hulled and
   sliced
Whipped cream

In medium bowl, toss strawberries with remaining ¼ cup sugar. Before serving, cut each shortcake in half crosswise. Top bottom half with strawberries and whipped cream. Cover with top half, more strawberries and whipped cream. Makes: about 8 shortcakes.

▼ Chocolate Almond Marble Pound Cake

Jinelles party 6-93

⅝ of 12-oz. pkg. (1¼ cups) Nestlé Toll House semi-sweet chocolate morsels, divided
3 cups all-purpose flour
2 teaspoons baking powder
½ teaspoon salt
1½ cups sugar
1 cup vegetable oil
¾ teaspoon almond extract
5 eggs
1 cup milk
Confectioners' sugar (optional)

Preheat oven to 350°F. Melt over hot (not boiling) water, ½ cup Nestlé Toll House semi-sweet chocolate morsels; stir until smooth. Set aside. In medium bowl, combine flour, baking powder and salt; set aside. In large bowl, combine sugar, vegetable oil and almond extract; beat well. Add eggs, 1 at a time, beating well after each addition. Gradually beat in flour mixture alternately with milk. Divide batter in half. Stir melted morsels and remaining ¾ cup Nestlé Toll House semi-sweet chocolate morsels into ½ of batter; mix well. Pour ½ of plain batter into greased and floured 10-inch tube pan. Top with ½ of chocolate batter. Repeat layers with remaining batters. Bake at: 350°F. for 65–70 minutes. Cool 15 minutes; remove from pan. Cool completely on wire rack. Sprinkle with confectioners' sugar, if desired. Makes: one tube cake.

◄ Bountiful Butterscotch Cake

One 12-oz. pkg. (2 cups)
    Nestlé Toll House
    butterscotch
    flavored morsels
¼ cup water
3 cups all-purpose flour
1 tablespoon baking
    powder
1 teaspoon salt
½ cup golden raisins
1 cup butter, softened
1 cup sugar
1 teaspoon vanilla
    extract
4 eggs
1 cup milk
½ cup finely chopped
    candied cherries
½ cup chopped toasted
    almonds
    Confectioners' sugar

Preheat oven to 350°F. Combine over hot (not boiling) water, Nestlé Toll House butterscotch flavored morsels and water. Stir until morsels are melted and mixture is smooth. Set aside. In medium bowl, combine flour, baking powder, salt and raisins; set aside. In large bowl, combine butter, sugar and vanilla extract; beat until creamy. Add eggs, 1 at a time, beating well after each addition. Gradually beat in flour mixture alternately with milk. Stir in butterscotch mixture, cherries and almonds. Pour into greased and floured 10-inch fluted tube pan. Bake at: 350°F. for 1 hour. Cool completely on wire rack; remove from pan. Sprinkle with confectioners' sugar. Garnish as desired. Makes: one tube cake.

Chocolate Orange Cake

4 cups all-purpose flour
2 teaspoons baking
    soda
½ teaspoon salt
2 cups sugar
1½ cups milk
1 cup vegetable oil
4 eggs
4 teaspoons vinegar
2 teaspoons vanilla
    extract
1 teaspoon grated
    orange rind
One 12-oz. pkg. (2 cups)
    Nestlé Toll House
    Little Bits semi-
    sweet chocolate

Cake: Preheat oven to 325°F. In medium bowl, combine flour, baking soda and salt; set aside. In large bowl, combine sugar, milk, vegetable oil, eggs, vinegar, vanilla extract and orange rind; beat well. Gradually beat in flour mixture. Stir in Nestlé Toll House Little Bits semi-sweet chocolate. Pour into greased and floured 10-inch fluted tube pan. Bake at: 325°F. for 65–70 minutes. Cool 10 minutes; remove from pan. Pierce cake evenly all over with toothpick. Brush cake with Glaze. Cool completely. Makes: one tube cake.

¼ cup orange juice
¼ cup sifted
    confectioners' sugar

Glaze: In small bowl, combine orange juice and confectioners' sugar; stir until blended.

Brownie Cream Chip Torte

One 12-oz. pkg. (2 cups)
Nestlé Toll House
Little Bits semi-
sweet chocolate,
divided
⅔ cup butter
1½ cups all-purpose flour
1 teaspoon baking
powder
½ teaspoon salt
4 eggs
1½ cups sugar
1 teaspoon vanilla
extract
½ cup chopped walnuts

Torte: Preheat oven to 350°F. Line bottom and sides of 15½×10½×1-inch baking pan with heavy duty foil; grease foil and set aside. Combine over hot (not boiling) water, ½ cup Nestlé Toll House Little Bits semi-sweet chocolate and butter. Stir until morsels are melted and mixture is smooth. Remove from heat; cool. In small bowl, combine flour, baking powder and salt; set aside. In large bowl, beat eggs and sugar until light and fluffy. Add cooled chocolate mixture; beat until well blended. Gradually blend in flour mixture. Stir in vanilla extract and walnuts. Spread batter into prepared pan. Bake at: 350°F. for 18–20 minutes. Loosen edges of cake; cool completely in pan. Invert onto cookie sheet; gently remove foil.

- -

2 cups heavy cream
¼ cup sifted
confectioners' sugar
1 teaspoon vanilla
extract
¾ cup Nestlé Toll House
Little Bits semi-
sweet chocolate,
reserved from 12-oz.
pkg.

Cream Chip Frosting: In medium bowl, combine heavy cream, confectioners' sugar and vanilla extract; beat until stiff. Fold in ¼ cup Nestlé Toll House Little Bits semi-sweet chocolate.

- -

¾ cup Nestlé Toll House
Little Bits semi-
sweet chocolate,
reserved from 12-oz.
pkg.

Trim edges of cake; cut cake crosswise into four 3¾×10-inch sections. Spread about ¾ cup Cream Chip Frosting on 1 layer. Top with second layer. Repeat layers of Frosting and cake. Frost entire cake with remaining Frosting. Garnish cake with remaining ¼ cup Nestlé Toll House Little Bits semi-sweet chocolate. Chill until ready to serve. Makes: one torte.

▲ Chocolate Mint Layer Cake

⅔ of 10-oz pkg. (1 cup)
  Nestlé Toll House
  mint-chocolate
  morsels
1¼ cups water, divided
2¼ cups all-purpose flour
  1 teaspoon salt
  1 teaspoon baking soda
  ½ teaspoon baking
    powder
1½ cups firmly packed
    brown sugar
  ½ cup butter, softened
  3 eggs
  Chocolate Mint
    Frosting (see pg. 58)

Preheat oven to 375°F. In small saucepan, combine Nestlé Toll House mint-chocolate morsels and ¼ cup water. Cook over medium heat, stirring constantly, until morsels are melted and mixture is smooth. Cool 10 minutes. In medium bowl, combine flour, salt, baking soda and baking powder; set aside. In large bowl, combine brown sugar and butter; beat until creamy. Add eggs, 1 at a time, beating well after each addition. Blend in chocolate mixture. Gradually beat in flour mixture alternately with remaining 1 cup water. Pour into 2 greased and floured 9-inch round baking pans. Bake at: 375°F. for 25–30 minutes. Cool completely on wire racks. Fill and frost with Chocolate Mint Frosting. Garnish as desired. Makes: one 2-layer cake.

◄ Toll House™ Cake

1 cup butter, softened
1 cup firmly packed
    brown sugar
⅔ cup sugar
4 eggs
2 teaspoons vanilla
    extract
½ teaspoon salt
2 cups all-purpose flour
One 12-oz. pkg. (2 cups)
    Nestlé Toll House
    Little Bits semi-
    sweet chocolate,
    divided

Cake: Preheat oven to 350°F. Grease bottom of 15½×10½×1-inch baking pan. Line with waxed paper; set aside. In large bowl, combine butter, brown sugar and sugar; beat until creamy. Add eggs, one at a time, beating well after each addition. Add vanilla extract and salt; mix well. Gradually add flour. Stir in 1 cup Nestlé Toll House Little Bits semi-sweet chocolate. Spread batter into prepared pan. Bake at: 350°F. for 20–25 minutes. Cool completely.

. . . .

1 cup Nestlé Toll House
    Little Bits semi-
    sweet chocolate,
    reserved from 12-oz.
    pkg.
¾ cup butter, softened
1½ cups sifted
    confectioners' sugar
2 teaspoons vanilla
    extract

Frosting: Melt over hot (not boiling) water, 1 cup Nestlé Toll House Little Bits semi-sweet chocolate; stir until smooth. Set aside. In small bowl, combine butter and confectioners' sugar; beat until creamy. Add melted chocolate and vanilla extract; blend until smooth.

. . . .

Loosen sides of cake. Invert onto lightly floured cloth. Peel off waxed paper. Trim edges of cake; cut cake crosswise into four 3¾×10-inch sections. Spread 3 slightly rounded tablespoonfuls Frosting on one cake layer. Top with second cake layer. Repeat layers of Frosting and cake. Frost entire cake with remaining Frosting. Makes: one cake.

Mocha Almond Torte

10 eggs, separated
2½ cups sifted
    confectioners' sugar
1 tablespoon Taster's
    Choice freeze dried
    coffee
2½ cups finely ground
    almonds

Cake: Preheat oven to 350°F. Grease 15½×10½×1-inch baking pan; line with waxed paper and grease paper. Set aside. In medium bowl, combine egg yolks, confectioners' sugar and Taster's Choice freeze dried coffee; beat until light and fluffy. In large bowl, beat egg whites until stiff peaks form. Gently fold in almonds. Fold in egg yolk mixture. Pour into prepared pan. Bake at: 350°F. for 30 minutes. Cake will spring back when touched lightly. Invert cake onto wire rack; remove waxed paper. Cool completely. Trim edges of cake. Cut into thirds lengthwise. Fill and frost with Mocha Frosting. Cake should be refrigerated. Makes: one cake.

2 teaspoons Taster's
    Choice freeze dried
    coffee
2 teaspoons boiling
    water
One 12-oz. pkg. (2 cups)
    Nestlé Toll House
    semi-sweet
    chocolate morsels
1 cup sweet butter,
    softened
2 eggs

Mocha Frosting: In small cup, dissolve Taster's Choice freeze dried coffee in boiling water; set aside. Melt over hot (not boiling) water, Nestlé Toll House semi-sweet chocolate morsels; stir until smooth. Set aside. In medium bowl, combine butter and eggs; beat until creamy. Beat in melted morsels. Add coffee; mix well.

Chocolate Fudge Cake

¾ of 12-oz. pkg. (1½
    cups) Nestlé Toll
    House semi-sweet
    chocolate morsels
1½ cups all-purpose flour
1 teaspoon baking soda
½ teaspoon salt
½ cup sugar
½ cup butter, softened
2 eggs
1 cup milk
1 tablespoon vinegar
    Chocolate
      Buttercream
      Frosting (see pg. 58)

Preheat oven to 350°F. Melt over hot (not boiling) water, Nestlé Toll House semi-sweet chocolate morsels; stir until smooth. Set aside. In small bowl, combine flour, baking soda and salt; set aside. In large bowl, combine sugar and butter; beat until creamy. Add eggs, 1 at a time, beating well after each addition.* Add melted morsels; mix until well blended. In small bowl, combine milk and vinegar; set aside. Gradually beat in flour mixture alternately with milk mixture. Spoon batter into two greased and floured 9-inch round baking pans. Bake at: 350°F. for 20–25 minutes. Cool 15 minutes; remove from pans. Cool completely on wire rack. Fill and frost with Chocolate Buttercream Frosting. Makes: one 2-layer cake.

*Mixture will appear curdled.

▲ Peanut Butter Cake

¼ of 12-oz. pkg. (½ cup)
  Nestlé Toll House
  peanut butter
  morsels
2 cups all-purpose flour
1 teaspoon baking soda
½ teaspoon baking
  powder
¼ teaspoon salt
½ cup butter, softened
1¼ cups sugar
2 eggs
1 teaspoon vanilla
  extract
1½ cups milk
  Peanut Butter Cream
  Frosting (see pg. 58)

Preheat oven to 350°F. Melt over hot (not boiling) water, ½ cup Nestlé Toll House peanut butter morsels; stir until smooth. Set aside. In medium bowl, combine flour, baking soda, baking powder and salt; set aside. In large bowl, combine butter and sugar; beat well. Blend in melted morsels. Beat in eggs and vanilla extract. Alternately blend in flour mixture and milk. Pour into 2 greased and floured 8-inch round cake pans. Bake at: 350°F. for 35–40 minutes. Cool 10 minutes; remove from pans. Cool completely on wire racks. Fill and frost with Peanut Butter Cream Frosting. Drizzle with melted chocolate morsels, if desired. Makes: one 2-layer cake.

FROSTINGS & TOPPINGS

Milk Chocolate Mallow Fudge Sauce ►

One 11½-oz. pkg. (2 cups) Nestlé Toll House milk chocolate morsels
2 cups miniature marshmallows
⅔ cup evaporated milk
3 tablespoons butter
1 teaspoon vanilla extract

Combine over hot (not boiling) water, Nestlé Toll House milk chocolate morsels, marshmallows, evaporated milk and butter. Stir until morsels and marshmallows are melted and mixture is smooth. Remove from heat; stir in vanilla extract. Serve warm over ice cream. Cover and store in refrigerator.*
Makes: about 2½ cups sauce.

Mocha Walnut Sauce ►

1 tablespoon Taster's Choice freeze dried coffee
1 tablespoon boiling water
½ cup heavy cream
½ cup sugar
One 6-oz. pkg. (1 cup) Nestlé Toll House semi-sweet chocolate morsels
½ cup butter
2 egg yolks
¾ cup chopped walnuts

In measuring cup, dissolve Taster's Choice freeze dried coffee in boiling water; set aside. In heavy gauge saucepan, combine heavy cream and sugar. Bring *just to boil*, stirring constantly, over medium heat. Add Nestlé Toll House semi-sweet chocolate morsels, butter and coffee; stir until smooth. Remove from heat. In small bowl, beat egg yolks. Gradually stir in 2 tablespoons chocolate mixture; mix well. Return to chocolate mixture in saucepan. Cook over low heat, stirring constantly, for 3 minutes; remove from heat. Stir in walnuts. Serve warm over ice cream. Cover and store in refrigerator.* Makes: 2¼ cups sauce.

*Reheat sauce over hot (not boiling) water before using OR microwave on high about 1 minute for each 1 cup sauce.

◄ Hot Peanut Butter
Ice Cream Sauce

½ of 12-oz. pkg. (1 cup)
    Nestlé Toll House
    peanut butter
    morsels
¾ cup corn syrup
¼ cup milk
2 tablespoons butter,
    softened
¼ teaspoon salt

In medium saucepan, combine Nestlé Toll House peanut butter morsels and corn syrup. Cook over low heat, stirring constantly, until morsels are melted and mixture is smooth. Add milk, butter and salt; stir until butter melts. Remove from heat; cool 5 minutes. Serve warm over ice cream. Cover and store in refrigerator.* Makes: 1⅔ cups sauce.

Chocolate Caramel Sauce

One 11½-oz. pkg. (2 cups)
    Nestlé Toll House
    milk chocolate
    morsels
10 caramels
¾ cup milk
2 tablespoons butter

In medium heavy gauge saucepan, combine Nestlé Toll House milk chocolate morsels, caramels, milk and butter. Cook over low heat, stirring constantly, until morsels and caramels are melted and mixture is smooth. Serve warm over ice cream. Cover and store in refrigerator.* Makes: about 2¼ cups sauce.

Note: Remaining sauce must be reheated.

Satiny Fudge Sauce

One 12-oz. pkg. (2 cups)
    Nestlé Toll House
    semi-sweet
    chocolate morsels
½ cup butter
2 cups miniature
    marshmallows
¾ cup milk

Combine over hot (not boiling) water, Nestlé Toll House semi-sweet chocolate morsels and butter. Stir until morsels are melted and mixture is smooth. Blend in marshmallows and milk. Cook, stirring constantly, until marshmallows are melted. Remove from heat; cool slightly. Serve warm over ice cream, pound cake or angel food cake. Cover and store in refrigerator.*
Makes: about 2¾ cups sauce.

*Reheat sauce over hot (not boiling) water before using OR microwave on high about 1 minute for each 1 cup sauce.

✓ 1.90 too rich

Chocolate Buttercream Frosting ▶

One 6-oz. pkg. (1 cup)
    Nestlé Toll House
    semi-sweet
    chocolate morsels
½ cup butter, softened
2 cups sifted
    confectioners' sugar
5 tablespoons milk
½ teaspoon vanilla
    extract*

Melt over hot (not boiling) water, Nestlé Toll House semi-sweet chocolate morsels; stir until smooth. Set aside; cool 15 minutes. In large bowl, beat butter until creamy. Gradually add confectioners' sugar alternately with milk. Add melted morsels and vanilla extract; beat until smooth. Fills and frosts Chocolate Fudge Cake (see pg. 52). Makes: 2⅓ cups frosting.

*½ teaspoon orange extract may be substituted.

Peanut Butter Cream Frosting ▶

½ of 12-oz. pkg. (1 cup)
    Nestlé Toll House
    peanut butter
    morsels
One 8-oz. pkg. cream
    cheese, softened
1 teaspoon vanilla
    extract
⅛ teaspoon salt
3 cups sifted
    confectioners' sugar
1 to 2 tablespoons milk

Melt over hot (not boiling) water, Nestlé Toll House peanut butter morsels; stir until smooth. Remove from heat. In large bowl, combine melted morsels, cream cheese, vanilla extract and salt; beat well. Beat in confectioners' sugar alternately with milk until mixture is spreading consistency. Fills and frosts Peanut Butter Cake (see pg. 53). Also excellent on chocolate layer cake.
Makes: about 2¼ cups frosting.

Chocolate Mint Frosting ▶

⅓ of 10-oz. pkg. (½ cup)
    Nestlé Toll House
    mint-chocolate
    morsels
¼ cup butter
1 teaspoon vanilla
    extract
¼ teaspoon salt
3 cups sifted
    confectioners' sugar
6 tablespoons milk

Combine over hot (not boiling) water, Nestlé Toll House mint-chocolate morsels and butter. Stir until morsels are melted and mixture is smooth. Stir in vanilla extract and salt. Transfer to large bowl. Gradually beat in confectioners' sugar alternately with milk; beat until smooth.* Fills and frosts Chocolate Mint Layer Cake (see pg. 49). Makes: about 2 cups frosting.

*If necessary, add more milk until desired consistency is reached.

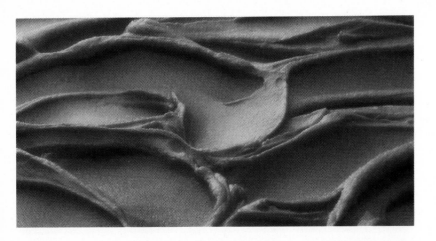

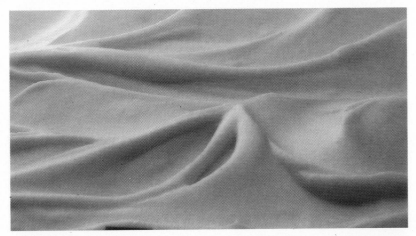

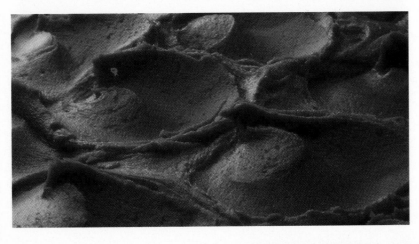

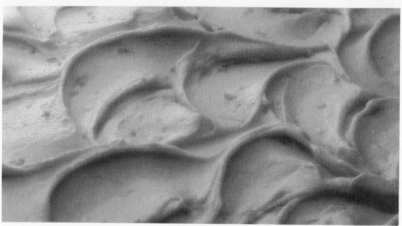

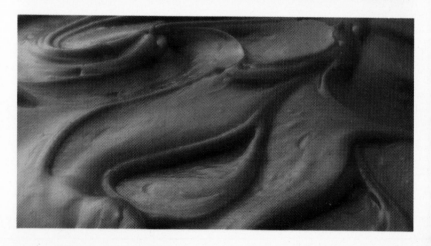

◄ Whipped Chocolate Cream Frosting

½ of 6-oz pkg. (½ cup)
  Nestlé Toll House
  semi-sweet
  chocolate morsels
½ cup heavy cream
1½ cups sifted
  confectioners' sugar
½ cup butter, softened
½ teaspoon vanilla
  extract

Combine over hot (not boiling) water, Nestlé Toll House semi-sweet chocolate morsels and heavy cream. Stir until morsels are melted and mixture is smooth. Set aside; chill thoroughly. In large bowl, combine confectioners' sugar, butter and vanilla extract; beat well. Gradually add chocolate mixture; beat until stiff. Delicious on chocolate or yellow layer cake; try on cupcakes. Makes: about 2⅓ cups frosting.

◄ Butterscotch Orange Frosting

One 6-oz. pkg. (1 cup)
  Nestlé Toll House
  butterscotch
  flavored morsels
½ cup butter, softened
2 cups sifted
  confectioners' sugar
¼ cup orange juice
1 tablespoon grated
  orange rind

Melt over hot (not boiling) water, Nestlé Toll House butterscotch flavored morsels; stir until smooth. Set aside; cool 15 minutes. In large bowl, beat butter until creamy. Gradually beat in confectioners' sugar alternately with orange juice. Stir in orange rind. Blend in melted morsels. Excellent on spice or yellow layer cake. Makes: 2⅓ cups frosting.

◄ Milk Chocolate Frosting

One 11½-oz. pkg. (2 cups)
  Nestlé Toll House
  milk chocolate
  morsels
6 tablespoons butter,
  softened
½ teaspoon salt
2½ cups sifted
  confectioners' sugar
¼ cup milk
1 teaspoon vanilla
  extract

Combine over hot (not boiling) water, Nestlé Toll House milk chocolate morsels, butter and salt. Stir until morsels are melted and mixture is smooth. Remove from heat and transfer to large bowl. Gradually beat in confectioners' sugar alternately with milk.* Beat in vanilla extract. Excellent on yellow or chocolate layer cake or cupcakes. Makes: 2½ cups frosting.

*If necessary, add more milk until desired consistency is reached.

BREADS

Chocolate and Cherry Braid ►

2¼ to 2¾ cups all-
  purpose flour,
  divided
2 pkgs. active dry yeast
⅔ cup milk
¼ cup sugar
2 tablespoons butter
½ teaspoon salt
1 egg
One 6-oz. pkg. (1 cup)
  Nestlé Toll House
  semi-sweet
  chocolate morsels
½ cup maraschino
  cherries, halved
1 egg yolk, beaten
  Toasted sliced
  almonds
  Candied cherries,
  halved

Bread: In large bowl, combine 1 cup flour and yeast. In small saucepan, combine ⅔ cup milk, sugar, butter and salt. Cook over medium heat, stirring constantly, until butter is almost melted (115°–120°F.). Add to flour mixture; beat until smooth. Add egg; mix well. Stir in Nestlé Toll House semi-sweet chocolate morsels, maraschino cherries and as much remaining flour as will mix in with spoon. Turn out onto lightly floured board. Knead in enough remaining flour to make a moderately stiff dough that is smooth and elastic (6–8 minutes). Divide dough into 3 equal pieces. Cover; let rest 10 minutes. Roll each piece into 18-inch rope. Braid loosely, beginning in middle and working toward ends. Press ends to seal and tuck under. Place on greased cookie sheet. Cover; place in refrigerator and let rise overnight. Remove from refrigerator and let stand 1 hour at room temperature. Preheat oven to 350°F. Brush bread with beaten egg yolk. Bake at: 350°F. for 30–35 minutes. Cool completely on wire rack. Drizzle with Glaze. Decorate with sliced almonds and candied cherries.
Makes: one braided loaf.

½ cup sifted
  confectioners' sugar
¼ teaspoon vanilla
  extract
2 teaspoons milk (about)

Glaze: In cup, combine confectioners' sugar, vanilla extract and enough milk to make Glaze of drizzling consistency.

▲ Little Bits™ Irish Soda Bread

4 cups all-purpose flour
¼ cup sugar
3 teaspoons baking powder
1 teaspoon baking soda
1 teaspoon salt
¼ cup butter, softened
1 cup golden raisins
¼ of 12-oz. pkg. (½ cup) Nestlé Toll House Little Bits semi-sweet chocolate
1⅓ cups buttermilk
1 egg
1 egg yolk
1 tablespoon water

Preheat oven to 375°F. In large bowl, combine flour, sugar, baking powder, baking soda and salt. Using pastry blender or 2 knives, cut in butter until mixture resembles coarse crumbs. Stir in raisins and Nestlé Toll House Little Bits semi-sweet chocolate. In small bowl, combine buttermilk and egg; beat well. Add to flour mixture; stir until dry ingredients are just moistened. On lightly floured board, knead dough (about 3 minutes). Shape into flattened ball. Place on lightly greased baking sheet. Score top of dough with sharp knife to form an x, about ½ inch deep. In cup, combine egg yolk and water. Brush on top of bread. Bake at: 375°F. for 50–60 minutes. Serve warm. Makes: one loaf.

Chocolate Banana Bread

1/3 cup raisins
3 tablespoons rum
1 1/2 cups all-purpose flour
1/2 teaspoon baking powder
1/2 teaspoon baking soda
1/2 teaspoon salt
1/2 cup sugar
1/2 cup mashed banana
1/4 cup butter, melted and cooled to room temperature
1 egg
2 tablespoons milk
1/2 of 6-oz. pkg. (1/2 cup) Nestlé Toll House semi-sweet chocolate morsels
1/4 cup chopped walnuts

In small bowl, combine raisins and rum. Let stand 15 minutes; drain and reserve liquid. Preheat oven to 350°F. In small bowl, combine flour, baking powder, baking soda and salt; set aside. In large bowl, combine sugar, banana, butter, egg and milk; beat well. Gradually beat in flour mixture. Stir in raisins, Nestlé Toll House semi-sweet chocolate morsels and nuts. Spread into greased and floured 8 1/2 × 4 1/2 × 2 1/2-inch loaf pan. Bake at: 350°F. for 45–50 minutes. Poke holes in top of bread with toothpick. Brush with reserved liquid. Cool 10 minutes; remove from pan. Cool completely on wire rack. Makes: one loaf.

Chocolate Apple Bread

2 teaspoons sugar
1/4 teaspoon cinnamon
1/4 cup finely chopped walnuts

Topping: In small cup, combine sugar, cinnamon and walnuts. Set aside.

2 cups all-purpose flour
1/2 teaspoon salt
1/2 teaspoon baking powder
1/2 teaspoon baking soda
1/2 teaspoon cinnamon
1/4 teaspoon nutmeg
1/2 cup butter, softened
1 cup sugar
2 eggs
1 teaspoon vanilla extract
2 tablespoons buttermilk
1 cup coarsely chopped apples
1/2 cup chopped walnuts
One 6-oz. pkg. (1 cup) Nestlé Toll House semi-sweet chocolate morsels

Bread: Preheat oven to 350°F. In medium bowl, combine flour, salt, baking powder, baking soda, cinnamon and nutmeg; set aside. In large bowl, combine butter and sugar; beat until creamy. Add eggs and vanilla extract; mix well. Gradually beat in flour mixture alternately with buttermilk. Stir in apples, walnuts and Nestlé Toll House semi-sweet chocolate morsels. Pour into greased 9 × 5 × 3-inch loaf pan. Sprinkle with Topping. Bake at: 350°F. for 50–60 minutes. Cool 15 minutes; remove from pan. Cool completely on wire rack. Makes: one loaf.

Granola Coffee Ring ►

One 6-oz. pkg. (1 cup)
    Nestlé Toll House
    butterscotch
    flavored morsels,
    divided
½ cup chopped nuts
½ teaspoon cinnamon

Filling: In small bowl, combine ½ cup Nestlé Toll House butterscotch flavored morsels, nuts and cinnamon. Set aside.

1 cup granola cereal
¾ cup sour cream
1¼ cups all-purpose flour
¾ teaspoon baking soda
¾ teaspoon baking
    powder
½ teaspoon salt
½ cup butter, softened
½ cup sugar
3 eggs
½ teaspoon grated
    orange rind
2 tablespoons finely
    chopped nuts

Cake: Preheat oven to 350°F. In large bowl, combine cereal and sour cream; let stand 15 minutes to soften cereal. In small bowl, combine flour, baking soda, baking powder and salt; set aside. Add butter, sugar, eggs and orange rind to granola/sour cream mixture; beat well. Gradually blend in flour mixture. Spoon ½ of batter into greased and floured 9-inch tube pan. Cover with Filling. Top with remaining batter. Bake at: 350°F. for 50 minutes. Cool cake 15 minutes. Remove from pan; cool completely on wire rack. Drizzle Glaze over top of cake. Sprinkle with nuts. Makes: one coffee ring.

½ cup Nestlé Toll House
    butterscotch
    flavored morsels,
    reserved from 6-oz.
    pkg.

Glaze: Melt over hot (not boiling) water, remaining ½ cup Nestlé Toll House butterscotch flavored morsels; stir until smooth.

Peanut Butter Surprise Muffins

½ of 12-oz. pkg. (1 cup)
    Nestlé Toll House
    peanut butter
    morsels
2 cups all-purpose flour
⅓ cup sugar
2½ teaspoons baking
    powder
½ teaspoon salt
2 tablespoons butter,
    softened
¾ cup milk
2 eggs, beaten
½ cup jam

Preheat oven to 400°F. Melt over hot (not boiling) water, Nestlé Toll House peanut butter morsels; stir until smooth. Set aside. In large bowl, combine flour, sugar, baking powder and salt. Add melted morsels and butter; stir until mixture resembles coarse crumbs. Add milk and eggs; stir until dry ingredients are just moistened. Spoon 1 rounded tablespoon batter into greased muffin cups; make well in center of each. Add 1½ teaspoonfuls jam in center. Spoon 2 rounded tablespoons batter on top; spread to cover completely. Bake at: 400°F. for 18–20 minutes. Cool 2 minutes; remove from pans to wire racks. Serve warm. Makes: 12 muffins.

Toll House™ Crumbcake ▼

1 tablespoon all-
   purpose flour
½ cup firmly packed
   brown sugar
2 tablespoons butter,
   softened
½ cup chopped nuts
One 12-oz. pkg. (2 cups)
   Nestlé Toll House
   Little Bits semi-
   sweet chocolate,
   divided

Topping: In small bowl, combine flour, brown sugar and butter; mix well. Stir in nuts and ½ cup Nestlé Toll House Little Bits semi-sweet chocolate; set aside.

2 cups all-purpose flour
1 teaspoon baking
   powder
1 teaspoon baking soda
½ teaspoon salt
½ cup butter, softened
1 cup sugar
1 teaspoon vanilla
   extract
3 eggs
1 cup sour cream
1½ cups Nestlé Toll House
   Little Bits semi-
   sweet chocolate,
   reserved from
   12-oz. pkg.

Cake: Preheat oven to 350°F. In small bowl, combine flour, baking powder, baking soda and salt; set aside. In large bowl, combine butter, sugar and vanilla extract; beat until creamy. Add eggs, one at a time, beating well after each addition. Gradually beat in flour mixture alternately with sour cream. Fold in remaining 1½ cups Nestlé Toll House Little Bits semi-sweet chocolate. Spread into greased 13×9-inch baking pan. Sprinkle Topping evenly over batter. Bake at: 350°F. for 45–50 minutes. Cool completely. Cut into 2-inch squares. Makes: 2 dozen squares.

▲ Chocolate Bubble Biscuits

2 cups all-purpose flour
¾ cup sugar, divided
4 teaspoons baking
powder
½ teaspoon salt
⅔ cup butter, divided
One 6-oz. pkg. (1 cup)
Nestlé Toll House
semi-sweet
chocolate morsels
⅔ cup milk
1 teaspoon cinnamon

In large bowl, combine flour, ¼ cup sugar, baking powder and salt. Using pastry blender or 2 knives, cut in ⅓ cup butter until mixture resembles coarse crumbs. Stir in Nestlé Toll House semi-sweet chocolate morsels. Add milk; stir until dough holds a shape. On floured board, knead dough *lightly*. Roll dough into 16 balls. Preheat oven to 375°F. In small saucepan, melt remaining ⅓ cup butter. Pour ½ of melted butter in 8-inch square baking pan. In cup, combine remaining ½ cup sugar and cinnamon. Sprinkle ⅓ cinnamon/sugar mixture over butter in baking pan. Place dough balls in single layer in pan. Brush with remaining melted butter. Sprinkle with remaining cinnamon/sugar mixture. Bake at: 375°F. for 30 minutes. Cool 10 minutes; remove from pan. Serve warm. Makes: 16 biscuits.

◄ Oatmeal Butterscotch Tea Biscuits

1 cup all-purpose flour
1 tablespoon baking
    powder
¾ teaspoon salt
¼ cup vegetable
    shortening
1 cup quick oats,
    uncooked
¾ of 6-oz. pkg. (¾ cup)
    Nestlé Toll House
    butterscotch
    flavored morsels
⅓ cup raisins
½ cup milk
1 egg
1 tablespoon honey
1 tablespoon sugar
¼ teaspoon cinnamon

Preheat oven to 425°F. In large bowl, combine flour, baking powder and salt. Using pastry blender or 2 knives, cut in shortening until mixture resembles coarse crumbs. Stir in oats, Nestlé Toll House butterscotch flavored morsels and raisins; set aside. In small bowl, combine milk, egg and honey; mix well. Add to flour mixture, stirring until dry ingredients are just moistened. Drop by rounded tablespoonfuls onto ungreased cookie sheets. In cup, combine sugar and cinnamon; sprinkle scant ¼ teaspoon over each biscuit. Bake at: 425°F. for 8–10 minutes.
Makes: about 1½ dozen biscuits.

Easy Chocolate Sweet Rolls

3 cups all-purpose flour,
    divided
2 pkgs. active dry yeast
1 teaspoon salt
½ teaspoon cinnamon
1¼ cups water
⅓ cup sugar
⅓ cup butter
1 egg
2 tablespoons grated
    orange rind
½ cup raisins
One 6-oz. pkg. (1 cup)
    Nestlé Toll House
    semi-sweet
    chocolate morsels

Rolls: In large bowl, combine 1½ cups flour, yeast, salt and cinnamon. In small saucepan, combine water, sugar and butter. Cook, stirring constantly, until butter is almost melted (115°–120°F.). Add to flour mixture; beat until smooth. Add egg and orange rind; beat well. Stir in remaining 1½ cups flour and raisins. Cover; let rise in warm place until almost doubled in bulk (about 1 hour). Stir down. Let stand 10 minutes. Stir in Nestlé Toll House semi-sweet chocolate morsels. Fill greased muffin cups ⅔ full. Cover; let rise in warm place until almost doubled in bulk (about 30 minutes). Preheat oven to 425°F. Bake at: 425°F. for 10–15 minutes. Cool completely; drizzle with Glaze.
Makes: about 1½ dozen rolls.

½ cup sifted
    confectioners' sugar
3 teaspoons orange
    juice

Glaze: In small bowl, combine confectioners' sugar and orange juice; beat until smooth.

Chocolate Pistachio Bread

1 pkg. active dry yeast
½ cup + 1 tablespoon
   sugar, divided
¼ cup warm water
   (105°–115°F.)
1 cup warm milk
   (105°–115°F.)
¼ cup butter, softened
2 teaspoons salt
4 cups all-purpose flour

Bread: In large bowl, combine yeast, 1 tablespoon sugar and water; let stand 10 minutes. Add milk, butter, salt and remaining ½ cup sugar; mix well. Stir in flour, 1 cup at a time, to form stiff dough. On lightly floured board, knead dough until smooth and elastic (about 10 minutes). Form into ball; place in greased bowl and turn once. Cover with plastic wrap; let rise in warm place until doubled in bulk (about 1 hour).

2 tablespoons butter,
   melted
1 cup coarsely chopped
   pistachio nuts
One 6-oz. pkg. (1 cup)
   Nestlé Toll House
   semi-sweet
   chocolate morsels
1 egg, beaten

Punch dough down and turn out on floured board. Roll into 18×12-inch rectangle; brush surface with melted butter. Sprinkle with pistachio nuts and Nestlé Toll House semi-sweet chocolate morsels. Roll up, jelly roll style, starting with long side. Shape into horseshoe; seal ends. Place seam side down on greased cookie sheet. Cover; let rise in warm place until doubled in bulk (about 30 minutes). Preheat oven to 375°F. Brush bread with beaten egg. Bake at: 375°F. for 30–35 minutes. Cool slightly. Drizzle Glaze over bread while still warm. Cool completely on wire rack. Makes: one horseshoe-shaped loaf.

½ cup sifted
   confectioners' sugar
3 teaspoons lemon juice

Glaze: In small bowl, combine confectioners' sugar and lemon juice; beat until smooth.

Chocolate Macadamia Muffins

¾ of 12-oz. pkg. (1½
   cups) Nestlé Toll
   House semi-sweet
   chocolate morsels
⅓ cup butter
1½ cups all-purpose flour
1 teaspoon baking soda
¼ teaspoon salt
1 cup chopped
   macadamia nuts
⅔ cup sour cream
¼ cup corn syrup
1 egg

Preheat oven to 375°F. Combine over hot (not boiling) water, Nestlé Toll House semi-sweet chocolate morsels and butter. Stir until morsels are melted and mixture is smooth. Set aside. In large bowl, combine flour, baking soda and salt. Add nuts and stir to coat well. Make well in center of flour mixture. In small bowl, combine melted morsels, sour cream, corn syrup and egg; mix until blended. Add to well in flour mixture; stir until just moistened. Spoon into paper-lined muffin cups, filling each about ¾ full. Bake at: 375°F. for 15–18 minutes. Cool 5 minutes; remove from pans. Cool completely on wire racks or serve warm. Makes: about 15 muffins.

1½ cups all-purpose flour
½ cup sugar
2 teaspoons baking
    powder
½ teaspoon cinnamon
½ teaspoon salt
1 cup milk
½ cup solid pack canned
    pumpkin
¼ cup butter, melted
1 egg
One 6-oz. pkg. (1 cup)
    Nestlé Toll House
    semi-sweet
    chocolate morsels
¼ cup finely chopped
    nuts

Preheat oven to 400°F. In large bowl, combine flour, sugar, baking powder, cinnamon and salt; make well in center. In small bowl, combine milk, pumpkin, butter and egg; add to well in flour mixture. Add Nestlé Toll House semi-sweet chocolate morsels; stir until dry ingredients are just moistened. Spoon mixture into greased muffin cups, filling each ¾ full. Sprinkle 1 teaspoon nuts over each muffin. Bake at: 400°F. for 18–20 minutes. Cool 5 minutes; remove from pans. Cool completely on wire racks. Makes: 12 muffins.

didn't pull from paper liners on bottom

CANDY

Creamy Chocolate Fudge ►

One 7-oz. jar marshmallow
cream
1½ cups sugar
⅔ cup evaporated milk
¼ cup butter
¼ teaspoon salt
One 11½-oz. pkg. (2 cups)
Nestlé Toll House
milk chocolate
morsels
One 6-oz. pkg. (1 cup)
Nestlé Toll House
semi-sweet
chocolate morsels
1 cup chopped walnuts
1 teaspoon vanilla
extract

In heavy gauge saucepan, combine marshmallow cream, sugar, evaporated milk, butter and salt. Bring to *full rolling boil* over medium heat, stirring constantly. *Boil 5 minutes*, stirring constantly. Remove from heat. Add Nestlé Toll House milk chocolate morsels and Nestlé Toll House semi-sweet chocolate morsels; stir until morsels are melted and mixture is smooth. Stir in walnuts and vanilla extract. Pour into foil-lined 8-inch square pan. Chill until firm (about 2 hours).
Makes: about 2½ pounds.

Prestige Pecan Drops ►

1 cup firmly packed
brown sugar
⅓ cup evaporated milk
2 tablespoons corn
syrup
One 6-oz. pkg. (1 cup)
Nestlé Toll House
semi-sweet
chocolate morsels
½ cup chopped pecans
1 teaspoon vanilla
extract
36 pecan halves

In heavy gauge saucepan, combine brown sugar, evaporated milk and corn syrup. Bring to *boil* over medium heat, stirring constantly. *Boil 2 minutes*, stirring constantly. Remove from heat. Add Nestlé Toll House semi-sweet chocolate morsels, chopped pecans and vanilla extract; stir until morsels are melted and mixture has thickened slightly. Drop by rounded teaspoonfuls onto waxed-paper-lined cookie sheet. Press pecan half on top. Chill until firm (about 30 minutes). Makes: 3 dozen candies.

▲ Ultimate Rocky Road

One 11½-oz. pkg. (2 cups) Nestlé Toll House milk chocolate morsels
2¼ cups miniature marshmallows
½ cup coarsely chopped nuts
¼ cup sunflower seeds

Melt over hot (not boiling) water, Nestlé Toll House milk chocolate morsels; stir until smooth. Remove from heat. Stir in marshmallows, nuts and sunflower seeds. Spread in foil-lined 8-inch square pan. Chill until firm (about 1 hour). Cut into 1-inch squares. Makes: about 5 dozen 1-inch squares.

▲ Macadamia Orange Fudge

3 cups sugar
¾ cup butter
⅔ cup evaporated milk
One 12-oz. pkg. (2 cups)
Nestlé Toll House
semi-sweet
chocolate morsels
One 7-oz. jar marshmallow
cream
1 cup macadamia nuts
2 tablespoons orange
flavored liqueur

In heavy gauge saucepan, combine sugar, butter and evaporated milk. Bring to *full rolling boil* over medium heat, stirring constantly. *Boil 5 minutes*, stirring constantly. Remove from heat. Add Nestlé Toll House semi-sweet chocolate morsels; stir until morsels are melted and mixture is smooth. Add marshmallow cream, nuts and orange flavored liqueur; beat until well blended. Pour into foil-lined 13×9-inch pan. Chill until firm (about 1–2 hours). Makes: about 2½ pounds.

◄ Butterscotch Fudge

1 cup finely chopped
   walnuts, divided
One 7-oz. jar marshmallow
   cream
1½ cups sugar
⅔ cup evaporated milk
¼ cup butter
¼ teaspoon salt
One 12-oz. pkg. (2 cups)
   Nestlé Toll House
   butterscotch
   flavored morsels
1 teaspoon orange
   extract
1 teaspoon grated
   orange rind

Foil-line 8-inch square pan. Spread ½ cup walnuts evenly on bottom of pan; set aside. In heavy gauge saucepan, combine marshmallow cream, sugar, evaporated milk, butter and salt. Bring to *full rolling boil* over medium heat, stirring constantly. *Boil* 5 *minutes*, stirring constantly. Remove from heat. Add Nestlé Toll House butterscotch flavored morsels; stir until morsels are melted and mixture is smooth. Stir in orange extract and orange rind. Pour into prepared pan. Sprinkle remaining ½ cup walnuts on top. Chill until firm (about 2 hours). Makes: about 2⅓ pounds.

◄ Chocolate Chip Eggnog Balls

Two 3-oz. pkgs. cream
   cheese, softened
4 cups sifted
   confectioners' sugar
1 tablespoon heavy
   cream
1 teaspoon brandy
   extract
½ teaspoon salt
¼ teaspoon cinnamon
⅛ teaspoon nutmeg
¼ of 12-oz. pkg. (½ cup)
   Nestlé Toll House
   Little Bits semi-
   sweet chocolate
1¼ cups finely chopped
   pecans

In large bowl, combine cream cheese, confectioners' sugar, heavy cream, brandy extract, salt, cinnamon and nutmeg; beat until creamy. Stir in Nestlé Toll House Little Bits semi-sweet chocolate. Drop by rounded teaspoonfuls onto cookie sheets. Chill 5 minutes. Roll into balls. Coat completely with nuts. Makes: about 3⅓ dozen balls.

Chocolate Amaretto Truffles ▼

One 11½-oz. pkg. (2 cups) Nestlé Toll House milk chocolate morsels
¼ cup sour cream
2 tablespoons almond flavored liqueur
⅔ cup finely chopped toasted almonds

Melt over hot (not boiling) water, Nestlé Toll House milk chocolate morsels; stir until smooth. Remove from heat. Blend in sour cream. Add almond flavored liqueur; mix well. Transfer to small bowl. Chill until firm. Drop by rounded teaspoonfuls onto waxed-paper-lined cookie sheets; shape into balls. Roll in almonds. Chill until firm (about 30 minutes). Makes: about 2½ dozen truffles.

Chocolate Creme de Mints ▲

One 11½-oz. pkg. (2 cups) Nestlé Toll House milk chocolate morsels
¼ cup sour cream
2½ tablespoons mint flavored liqueur

Melt over hot (not boiling) water, Nestlé Toll House milk chocolate morsels; stir until smooth. Remove from heat. Blend in sour cream. Stir in mint flavored liqueur. Transfer to small bowl. Chill until thickened (about 30 minutes). Fill pastry bag fitted with decorative tip; pipe 1-inch candies onto foil-lined cookie sheets. Chill until ready to serve.
Makes: about 3½ dozen candies.

▲Chocolate-Dipped Fruit

One 11½-oz. pkg. (2 cups)
  Nestlé Toll House
  milk chocolate
  morsels
¼ cup vegetable
  shortening
Fresh fruit, rinsed,
  patted dry
Canned fruit, drained,
  patted dry

Combine over hot (not boiling) water, Nestlé Toll House milk chocolate morsels and vegetable shortening. Stir until morsels are melted and mixture is smooth. Remove from heat but keep over hot water. (If chocolate begins to set, return to heat. Add 1–2 teaspoons vegetable shortening; stir until smooth.) Dip pieces of fruit into chocolate mixture, shaking off excess. Place on foil-lined cookie sheets. Chill until set (about 10–15 minutes). Gently loosen from foil with metal spatula. Chocolate-Dipped Fruit may be kept at room temperature up to 1 hour. If chocolate becomes sticky, return to refrigerator.
Makes: 1 cup melted chocolate.

▲ Peanut Butter & Jelly Crisps

One 12-oz. pkg. (2 cups)
Nestlé Toll House
peanut butter
morsels
2 tablespoons vegetable
shortening
½ cup jam or jelly
60 round buttery crackers

Combine over hot (not boiling) water, Nestlé Toll House peanut butter morsels and vegetable shortening. Stir until morsels are melted and mixture is smooth. Remove from heat but keep over hot water. Spread 1 scant teaspoon jam on flat side of 1 cracker; top with another cracker. Repeat with remaining crackers. Chill for 15 minutes. Dip each sandwich into melted morsels; shake off excess. Place on waxed-paper-lined cookie sheets. Chill until set (about 30 minutes). Makes: 30 crisps.

◄ Peanut Butter Balls

One 12-oz. pkg. (2 cups)
Nestlé Toll House
peanut butter
morsels
⅓ cup evaporated milk
¼ cup butter
2 eggs, slightly beaten
1 teaspoon vanilla
extract
2 cups sifted
confectioners' sugar
One 3½-oz. can (1⅓ cups)
flaked coconut,
divided
1 cup chopped peanuts,
divided

Combine over hot (not boiling) water, Nestlé Toll House peanut butter morsels, evaporated milk and butter. Stir until morsels are melted and mixture is smooth. Stir in eggs; cook 2 minutes longer. Blend in vanilla extract and confectioners' sugar. Stir in ¾ cup coconut and ½ cup peanuts. Transfer to large bowl. Chill until firm enough to handle (about 2 hours). Using 1 rounded teaspoonful, shape into balls. In small bowl, combine remaining coconut and peanuts. Roll balls into nut mixture. Place on waxed-paper-lined cookie sheets. Chill until firm (about 1 hour). Makes: about 3½ dozen candies.

Chocolate Cherry Almond Drops

One 12-oz. pkg. (2 cups)
Nestlé Toll House
semi-sweet
chocolate morsels
¾ cup chopped candied
red cherries
1 cup chopped toasted
almonds

Melt over hot (not boiling) water, Nestlé Toll House semi-sweet chocolate morsels; stir until smooth. Stir in cherries and almonds. Drop by rounded teaspoonfuls onto waxed-paper-lined cookie sheet. Chill until firm (about 30 minutes). Store in airtight container in refrigerator. Makes: about 2½ dozen candies.

DESSERTS

Chocolate Filled Cream Puff Ring ▶

1 cup water
½ cup butter
1 cup all-purpose flour
4 eggs

Cream Puff Ring: Preheat oven to 400°F. In medium saucepan, combine water and butter. Bring to *boil* over low heat. Gradually add flour, stirring constantly until mixture cleans the sides of pan. Remove from heat. Add eggs, 1 at a time, beating well after each addition. Drop by 2 rounded tablespoonfuls onto ungreased cookie sheet, connecting to form circle. Bake at: 400°F. for 35–40 minutes. Cool completely. Slice cream puffs in half horizontally. Fill with Filling. Cover with top half. Drizzle with Glaze. Makes: 8 servings.

⅔ of 12-oz. pkg. (1⅓ cups) Nestlé Toll House semi-sweet chocolate morsels, divided
Two 3-oz. pkgs. cream cheese, softened
½ cup sifted confectioners' sugar
1 tablespoon raspberry flavored liqueur (optional)
½ cup heavy cream, whipped

Filling: Melt over hot (not boiling) water, 1 cup Nestlé Toll House semi-sweet chocolate morsels; stir until smooth. Set aside. In medium bowl, combine cream cheese, confectioners' sugar and raspberry flavored liqueur; beat until creamy. Gradually add melted morsels; beat well. Fold in whipped cream.

⅓ cup Nestlé Toll House semi-sweet chocolate morsels, reserved from 12-oz. pkg.
1 tablespoon vegetable shortening

Glaze: Combine over hot (not boiling) water, remaining ⅓ cup Nestlé Toll House semi-sweet chocolate morsels and vegetable shortening. Stir until morsels are melted and mixture is smooth.

▲ Heavenly Chocolate Cheesecake

**2 cups vanilla wafers,
finely crushed**
**1 cup ground toasted
almonds**
½ cup butter, melted
½ cup sugar

Crust: In large bowl, combine vanilla wafer crumbs, almonds, butter and sugar; mix well. Pat firmly into 9-inch springform pan, covering bottom and 2 inches up sides; set aside.

**One 11½-oz. pkg: (2 cups)
Nestlé Toll House
milk chocolate
morsels**
½ cup milk
**1 envelope unflavored
gelatin**
**Two 8-oz. pkgs. cream
cheese, softened**
½ cup sour cream
**½ teaspoon almond
extract**
**½ cup heavy cream,
whipped**

Cake: Melt over hot (not boiling) water, Nestlé Toll House milk chocolate morsels; stir until smooth. Set aside. Pour milk into small saucepan; sprinkle gelatin on top. Set aside for 1 minute. Cook over low heat, stirring constantly, until gelatin dissolves. Set aside. In large bowl, combine cream cheese, sour cream and melted morsels; beat until fluffy. Beat in gelatin mixture and almond extract. Fold in whipped cream. Pour into prepared pan. Chill until firm (about 3 hours). Run knife around edge of cake to separate from pan; remove sides. Garnish as desired.
Makes: one cheesecake.

Chocolate Almond Frozen Mousse

One 6-oz. pkg. (1 cup)
Nestlé Toll House
semi-sweet
chocolate morsels
3 egg yolks
1/4 cup coffee flavored
liqueur (optional)
1/8 teaspoon salt
1 cup heavy cream,
whipped
2/3 cup chopped toasted
almonds, divided

Mousse: Melt over hot (not boiling) water, Nestlé Toll House semi-sweet chocolate morsels; stir until smooth. Transfer to large bowl; cool 10 minutes. Using wire whisk, quickly blend in egg yolks, coffee flavored liqueur and salt. Fold in whipped cream. Pour 1/2 of mixture into foil-lined 3-cup bowl. Spoon 1/3 cup almonds on top; top with remaining chocolate mixture. Freeze 3 hours or until firm. Unmold onto serving dish; remove foil. Decorate mousse with Topping and remaining 1/3 cup almonds. Let mousse stand at room temperature 10 minutes before serving. Makes: six 1/2-cup servings.

2/3 cup heavy cream
2 tablespoons sifted
confectioners' sugar
1 teaspoon vanilla
extract

Topping: In small bowl, combine heavy cream, confectioners' sugar and vanilla extract; beat until stiff.

Brandy Alexander Gems

Pastry for one crust
9-inch pie

Gem Cups: Preheat oven to 450°F. Cut pastry into 24 circles using 2½-inch round cookie cutter. Press circle in each cup of gem pans.* Bake at: 450°F. for 7–9 minutes. Remove from pans. Cool completely on wire racks.

1/3 of 12-oz. pkg. (2/3 cup)
Nestlé Toll House
Little Bits semi-
sweet chocolate,
divided
1/3 cup heavy cream
1/4 cup sugar
1/8 teaspoon salt
2 egg yolks
1 tablespoon brandy
Whipped cream

Filling: In small heavy gauge saucepan, combine 1/2 cup Nestlé Toll House Little Bits semi-sweet chocolate, heavy cream, sugar and salt. Cook over low heat, stirring constantly, until chocolate is melted and mixture is smooth. Remove from heat. In small bowl, beat egg yolks. Stir in 1/4 cup chocolate mixture. Return to saucepan; cook 1 minute longer. Stir in brandy. Pour into Gem Cups. Chill. Serve with whipped cream; sprinkle with remaining Nestlé Toll House Little Bits semi-sweet chocolate. Makes: 24 gems.

*Gem pans are miniature muffin pans.

½ of 11½-oz. pkg. (1 cup) Nestlé Toll House milk chocolate morsels
One 15-oz. container ricotta cheese
Two 3-oz. pkgs. cream cheese, softened
2 tablespoons sifted confectioners' sugar
2 tablespoons chopped citron
1 teaspoon vanilla extract
12 prepared 5-inch cannoli shells
⅓ cup finely chopped pistachio nuts

Melt over hot (not boiling) water, Nestlé Toll House milk chocolate morsels; stir until smooth. Remove from heat; cool to room temperature. In small bowl, beat ricotta cheese until smooth. Add cream cheese, confectioners' sugar, citron and vanilla extract; beat well. Blend in melted morsels. Spoon into cannoli shells. Dip ends in nuts. Chill until ready to serve. Makes: 12 cannolis.

▲ Chocolate Meringue Cups with Chocolate Sauce

3 egg whites
⅛ teaspoon cream of tartar
⅛ teaspoon salt
1 cup sifted confectioners' sugar
1 teaspoon vanilla extract
One 12-oz. pkg. (2 cups) Nestlé Toll House Little Bits semisweet chocolate, divided
Ice cream

Chocolate Meringue Cups: Draw twelve 2-inch circles 1 inch apart on parchment-paper-lined cookie sheet. Set aside. Preheat oven to 300°F. In large bowl, combine egg whites, cream of tartar and salt; beat until soft peaks form. Gradually add confectioners' sugar and vanilla extract; beat until stiff peaks form. Fold in 1 cup Nestlé Toll House Little Bits semi-sweet chocolate. Spoon meringue into 12 circles, making well in center of each one. Bake at: 300°F. for 25 minutes. Turn oven off. Let stand in oven with door ajar 30 minutes. Remove from paper. Serve with scoop of ice cream and Chocolate Sauce.
Makes: 12 meringue cups and 1¼ cups sauce.

- -

1 cup Nestlé Toll House Little Bits semisweet chocolate, reserved from 12-oz. pkg.
½ cup heavy cream
2 tablespoons butter
¼ cup raspberry flavored liqueur

Chocolate Sauce: Combine over hot (not boiling) water, remaining 1 cup Nestlé Toll House Little Bits semi-sweet chocolate, heavy cream and butter. Stir until morsels are melted and mixture is smooth. Stir in raspberry flavored liqueur. Serve warm or chilled.

Chocolate Mint Ice Cream ►

1½ cups heavy cream,
     divided
1 cup milk
⅓ cup sugar
One 10-oz. pkg. (1½ cups)
     Nestlé Toll House
     mint-chocolate
     morsels, divided
2 egg yolks
⅛ teaspoon salt

In heavy gauge saucepan, combine 1¼ cups heavy cream, milk, sugar and 1 cup Nestlé Toll House mint-chocolate morsels. Cook over low heat, stirring with wire whisk, until morsels are melted and mixture is smooth. Remove from heat. In medium bowl, beat egg yolks and salt until thick. Gradually add chocolate mixture; beat until well blended. Chill 30 minutes. In small heavy gauge saucepan, combine remaining ½ cup Nestlé Toll House mint-chocolate morsels and ¼ cup heavy cream. Cook over low heat, stirring constantly, until morsels are melted and mixture is smooth. Remove from heat; set aside. Pour chilled chocolate/egg mixture into electric ice cream freezer; churn until thick (about 25 minutes). Pour in reserved chocolate mixture; churn 10 seconds. Remove dasher; cover and store in freezer until ready to serve. Makes: 1 quart.

Toll House™ Quick Ice Cream ►

½ cup + 2 tablespoons
     firmly packed brown
     sugar
½ cup butter
3 eggs
2 teaspoons vanilla
     extract
½ teaspoon salt
2 cups heavy cream
½ of 12-oz. pkg. (1 cup)
     Nestlé Toll House
     Little Bits semi-
     sweet chocolate
1 cup chopped toasted
     walnuts

In small heavy gauge saucepan, combine brown sugar and butter. Bring to *boil* over low heat, stirring occasionally; *boil* 1 minute. Remove from heat. In blender container, combine eggs, vanilla extract and salt; cover and blend at medium speed for 30 seconds. Gradually pour in brown sugar mixture; blend at high speed for 1 minute. Set aside; cool to room temperature. In large bowl, beat heavy cream until stiff. Fold in butter/sugar mixture. Fold in Nestlé Toll House Little Bits semi-sweet chocolate and walnuts. Pour into foil-lined 9×5×3-inch loaf pan. Cover with foil; freeze until firm (several hours or overnight). Makes: about 1½ quarts.

▲ Frozen Chocolate Soufflé Cordial

¾ of 12-oz. pkg. (1½ cups) Nestlé Toll House semi-sweet chocolate morsels
2 cups heavy cream, divided
1 cup sifted confectioners' sugar
¼ cup milk
6 eggs, separated
½ cup coffee flavored liqueur
2 tablespoons sugar
2 tablespoons ground toasted almonds

Prepare 2-inch foil collar for 1½-quart soufflé dish. Set aside. Combine over hot (not boiling) water, Nestlé Toll House semi-sweet chocolate morsels, ¼ cup heavy cream, confectioners' sugar and milk. Stir until morsels are melted and mixture is smooth. Remove from heat. In small bowl, beat egg yolks until thick. Stir into chocolate mixture. Return to heat. Cook over low heat, stirring constantly, until mixture thickens slightly (about 8–10 minutes). Remove from heat; stir in coffee flavored liqueur. Transfer to large bowl; chill until mixture thickens slightly. In large bowl, beat remaining 1¾ cups heavy cream until stiff. Set aside. In medium bowl, beat egg whites until foamy; gradually beat in sugar until stiff peaks form. Fold egg whites and whipped cream into chocolate mixture. Pour into prepared dish. Sprinkle with almonds. Freeze 5–6 hours. Remove collar. Allow to stand at room temperature 30 minutes before serving. Makes: 12 servings.

Chocolate Swirl Bavarian

2 envelopes unflavored gelatin
⅓ cup water
1 cup sugar, divided
¼ cup cornstarch
¼ teaspoon salt
2 cups milk, scalded
4 eggs, separated
One 12-oz. pkg. (2 cups) Nestlé Toll House semi-sweet chocolate morsels, divided
¼ teaspoon almond extract
1 cup heavy cream, whipped

In small bowl, combine gelatin and water; set aside. In large saucepan, combine ½ cup sugar, cornstarch and salt. Gradually stir in scalded milk. In small bowl, beat egg yolks with fork. Add some of hot milk mixture to egg yolks; mix well. Return to mixture in saucepan. Cook over medium heat, stirring constantly, until mixture thickens (about 5 minutes). Add softened gelatin; stir until gelatin dissolves. Transfer 1¼ cups custard to bowl. Add 1½ cups Nestlé Toll House semi-sweet chocolate morsels; stir until morsels are melted and mixture is smooth. Transfer remaining custard to another bowl; stir in almond extract. Cover surface of both custards with plastic wrap. Cool to room temperature. In 1½-quart bowl, beat egg whites until foamy. Gradually add remaining ½ cup sugar, beating until stiff peaks form. Fold ½ of egg whites and ½ of whipped cream into chocolate custard. Fold remaining egg whites and whipped cream into almond custard. Divide almond mixture among eight 6-ounce dessert molds. Spoon chocolate custard into pastry bag fitted with wide tip. Insert tip into center of almond mixture. Pipe chocolate mixture into almond mixture until level reaches top of mold. Chill several hours until firm. To unmold: Loosen edge of mold with metal spatula. Set mold in pan of hot water for 10 seconds. Place serving plate over mold and invert. Melt over hot (not boiling) water, remaining ½ cup Nestlé Toll House semi-sweet chocolate morsels; stir until smooth. Drizzle melted chocolate over each serving.
Makes: 8 Bavarians.

Mocha Chocolate Chip Cheesecake

2¼ cups graham cracker crumbs

One 12-oz. pkg. (2 cups) Nestlé Toll House Little Bits semi-sweet chocolate, divided

⅔ cup butter, melted and cooled to room temperature

Crust: In large bowl, combine graham cracker crumbs, 1 cup Nestlé Toll House Little Bits semi-sweet chocolate and butter; mix well. Pat firmly into 9-inch springform pan, covering bottom and 2½ inches up sides. Set aside.

. . . .

½ cup milk

4 teaspoons Taster's Choice freeze dried coffee

1 envelope unflavored gelatin

Two 8-oz. pkgs. cream cheese, softened

One 14-oz. can sweetened condensed milk

2 cups heavy cream, whipped

1 cup Nestlé Toll House Little Bits semi-sweet chocolate, reserved from 12-oz. pkg.

Cake: In small saucepan, combine milk and Taster's Choice freeze dried coffee; sprinkle gelatin on top. Set aside for 1 minute. Cook over low heat, stirring constantly, until gelatin and coffee dissolve. Set aside. In large bowl, beat cream cheese until creamy. Beat in sweetened condensed milk and gelatin mixture. Fold in whipped cream and remaining 1 cup Nestlé Toll House Little Bits semi-sweet chocolate. Pour into prepared Crust. Chill until firm (about 2 hours). Run knife around edge of cake to separate from pan; remove sides. Makes: one cheesecake.

Fudgy Rice Pudding Supreme

6 cups milk

¾ cup uncooked white rice

¼ cup sugar

¼ teaspoon salt

½ of 11½-oz. pkg. (1 cup) Nestlé Toll House milk chocolate morsels

2 teaspoons vanilla extract

1 cup heavy cream, whipped

¼ teaspoon cinnamon

In large saucepan, combine milk, rice, sugar and salt. Cook over medium heat, stirring constantly, until mixture starts to *boil*. Reduce heat; cover and simmer 45 minutes or until rice is tender, stirring occasionally. Add Nestlé Toll House milk chocolate morsels and vanilla extract; stir until morsels are melted. Transfer to large bowl; cover. Chill thoroughly (about 2 hours). Fold in whipped cream. Spoon into dessert dishes. Sprinkle with cinnamon. Makes: nine ½-cup servings.

▲ Little Bits™
Baked Pancake with Fruit

¼ cup butter
4 eggs
1 cup milk
1 cup all-purpose flour
½ of 12-oz. pkg. (1 cup)
    Nestlé Toll House
    Little Bits semi-
    sweet chocolate
2 cups fresh fruit
    Confectioners' sugar

Preheat oven to 425°F. In oven, melt butter in 10-inch cast iron skillet. In large bowl, combine eggs, milk and flour; beat until foamy. Pour into hot skillet. Bake at: 425°F. for 2 minutes. Remove from oven. Sprinkle Nestlé Toll House Little Bits semi-sweet chocolate over pancake. Return to oven. Bake at: 425°F. for 17–19 minutes. Top with fresh fruit and sprinkle with confectioners' sugar. Serve immediately. Makes: one pancake.

INDEX